Soul Sanctum

By

John Gibson

WORDS MATTER
P U B L I S H I N G
OUR WORDS CHANGE THE WORLD

Words Matter Publishing
P.O. Box 1190
Decatur, IL 62525
www.wordsmatterpublishing.com

ISBN: 978-1-958000-84-7

Library of Congress Catalog Card Number: 2023946309

DEDICATION

This book is dedicated to the students at Vernon High School, whom I am proud to have called my students.

ACKNOWLEDGMENTS

Thanks, as always, to my wife, Melissa, for her love, support, and encouragement. And also, for helping edit the book. Thanks also to Mrs. Rhonda Dickinson for her expertise in helping edit as well!

TABLE OF CONTENTS

CHAPTER 1

Yearwood, Kentucky – August 2019

As I trailed behind Jamie, I was reminded once more of how grown he was getting…and how old I was becoming. No longer was my son the little squirt who tagged along with me to practices and games wherever I may have been coaching. He was a teenager now, on the cusp of starting his football career in high school.

Soon, James Soulemain Leonard would be a man, and I was not ready for this.

He beat me to the top of the stadium steps, and right away began doing his version of a victory dance as he raised his arms in the air, throwing a series of air punches.

"You don't stop gloatin' and I'll gut-punch you," I wheezed as I made it to the top right behind him.

He grinned at me, his wry smile and sidelong glance reminding me of that moment of my own mother's. Jamie was like most kids; a near-seamless amalgamation of both sides of his family. There were moments when the two of us only had to walk side-by-side for everyone to know that we were father and son. Then at other times, I'd swear he was the spitting image of his mother.

"Weak as you look, that punch would barely feel like a poke," he quipped back at me.

I managed a faint laugh. It was the dry wit he had inherited from his mother.

"Good Soul Sprint," he said, offering me his fist.

I bumped it, and returned, "Good Soul Sprint."

We caught our breath as we stood at the top of Mustang Stadium, gazing down at the field. Located on the campus of Yearwood State University, the field was my current coaching venue, a fact that guaranteed Jamie and me the right to use the facilities any time we wished. Football field, track, weight room; Jamie's access to it all was one reason why he was now competing for a starting position on his varsity football roster as a ninth-grader.

Once the two of us were both standing upright again, I spoke. "Big day tomorrow."

"Big practice," Jamie nodded, wiping sweat from his brow. "We'll find out who the quarterback's going to be."

"How are you feeling?" I prodded. "Nervous?"

Jamie shrugged. "A little…I feel pretty good about it, though."

It was exactly the type of response that I had come to expect from my only son. In addition to his mother's sense of humor, he had also inherited her sense of cool, calm self-assurance and moxie with which she approached every situation.

But then he also reminded me of the two men after whom he had been named: Jamie Gill, my best friend from my hometown of Lake Barrow, and Soulemain Rasheed, my best friend from college.

He wore both names well.

"Hard to beat out an upperclassman," I told Jamie, as we continued our morning ritual, walking part of the perimeter of the uppermost stadium level.

Jamie seemed to brush off my remark. "Paul's talented," he said. "But his mechanics are off. Coach even said so."

And that was my influence. Jamie knew more about playing the position of quarterback just from hanging around with me than most of his peers ever would.

"He seems like he gets flustered, too," I said, as we neared the press box.

"Yeah," Jamie agreed, using the shirttail of his "Yearwood Football" gray t-shirt to wipe his brow and push his blonde curly bangs out of his face. "Coach Richroath will mess you up if you let him. Paul lets him get into his head too much."

I chuckled. "He definitely will," I said to Jamie. "Can't believe he's still coaching; the man's gotta be approaching seventy."

"Wasn't he the coach when you played college ball here?" Jamie asked.

I nodded. "He used to have me come out and do camps with his players when I was quarterback," I reminisced. "Always laughed at me, though; said I was too soft on the players; said I'd never be a coach."

Both of us laughed at the irony.

"What's funny," I continued, "is he hasn't asked me to do a single camp since we moved here in 2017. Here I am now, the offensive coordinator of the Yearwood State Mustangs, my college team, and still no invitation. He must really think I suck at coaching."

Jamie chuckled. "Or he just doesn't want to admit that he was wrong about you."

"Maybe so," I rejoined.

We continued, as the sun began its peeking ascent over the home side stands of our stadium.

"Proud of you, Jamie," I told him.

He grinned, with a 'yeah-whatever' expression on his face, but there was just enough sincerity in his smile to let me know that he still valued my affirmation. I hoped he always would.

"I'm gonna head down," he told me after a few moments.

"Milo on his way?" I asked.

Jamie smiled again. "You know it," he responded. "Should be here any minute."

The sun was still rising in the east, as I watched my only son head down to meet his good friend for a game of catch.

My heart beamed as I watched him go.

"Whaddya say, Milo!" I called ten minutes later from the goal line, as Jamie and a smaller boy with Down Syndrome walked through the tunnel and onto the field.

Milo Crenshaw's round face lit up when he saw me. "Coach Jayce!" he exclaimed, raising his arms. "How's the championship team?"

"We're gettin' there," I answered. "You come run the ball for us, we might just get that championship."

Milo giggled as he lumbered his stocky frame toward me and gave me a jump-in-the-air high-five. "I can run that ball!" he said.

"I know you can," I affirmed.

To know Milo Crenshaw was to know a soul who kept right on smiling, and right on loving, and right on living, no matter what life threw at him. And at the age of fourteen, life had already thrown a lot.

"How'd the doctor's appointment go last week?" I asked him.

"Eh," Milo said. "This heart's not too good," he said, touching his chest. "But at least my real heart is good; the one God looks at, like Nanny says."

"Nanny doing well?" I asked.

Milo nodded. "She takes care of me," he replied. "And you all help."

"We do what we can," I told him.

"Thank you!" he said with another bright smile.

Down Syndrome, heart trouble – the kind which could one day become fatal - abandonment as a baby, and having to live with a grandmother with health problems of her own. I had never seen any of those major life problems dim Milo Crenshaw's ebullient smile or unwaveringly positive spirit. Nor, for that matter, had it ever dampened his devotion to the Yearwood State Mustangs.

Milo and Jamie had become friends in seventh grade, and that friendship had continued as they both prepared to start high school. I watched as the two of them began to throw the football and wondered just how many relationships like theirs had fallen by the wayside due to peer pressure. Cliquishness and adherence to an unwritten social code were no secret in the halls of middle and high school. Kids who were vastly different from each other often went to great lengths to avoid each other altogether. And yet, Jamie and Milo's friendship had persisted with a strength all its own.

Like me, Jamie had played sports throughout his childhood years. Unlike me, Jamie had never allowed his status as an athlete to define his friendships.

At age fifteen, my son was perhaps a better man than I ever would be.

For a few minutes, I watched as Jamie lobbed sideline passes to his friend in the end zone for a few moments. Milo caught only a few of them, but after each one that he did catch, did his own jerky celebration dance in the end zone.

I smiled as I turned and began scanning the field known as "Mustang Stadium," and it occurred to me once more that this stadium was, for me, much more than an athletic venue. It was a sanctuary…for the soul.

Soul.

This field, on which I had played quarterback as a collegian, and had now come back to as an assistant head coach, contained a memory on each hash mark, it seemed. It was as if the fading white paint of each yard line somehow conjured up a fuzzy home movie as I turned my eyes upon each one.

Most of those memories involved Soul Rasheed.

He and I—myself at quarterback, and he as my top receiver— had combined on more clutch third-down-and-long touchdowns than I could remember. And yet, a few of them jumped out at me like ghosts as I scanned the horizons of the field.

Our own thirty-five-yard line. *Indiana University.* The 2000 season. Soul had gone up between two defenders for a mid-range pass over the middle and had been sandwiched by both as he held onto the ball. It was the fourth quarter, and we were driving. That catch had enabled a game-winning field goal.

2001; the Louisville game, which went to overtime. To be precise, Soul and I had *sent* it to overtime on a twenty-five-yard sideline pass that sealed the tie with the extra point.

Soul had been the perfect receiver; large, strong, fast – able to beat a defender with downfield speed just as easily as he could fight him off for a hanging, arcing pass that was going to land in someone's hands. Soul usually won those battles and had for sure won that one, as he caught the ball in the endzone. The crowd had erupted into a frenzy, as we almost knocked off the University of Louisville on our turf.

Louisville. Not all of the memories were pleasant.

A year later, our senior year, we were playing Louisville again; this time on their home field. It was that game that had ended both the season and the career of Soul Rasheed. He had scored on a long touchdown, and had been carted off the field moments later, after a Louisville defender – angry that Soul had gotten the better of him on that last play – ran up and hit him from behind in the end zone after the play had been whistled dead. Soul's knee was destroyed, as were his playing days.

But not his spirit.

Soul had gone on to be a graduate assistant with me at Yearwood State. From there, he had followed me to my hometown of Lake Barrow, where I became the youngest head coach–at the time—in the state of Florida at my high school alma mater. There, Soul had served as my assistant coach and offensive coordinator for the Spartans of Sims County High School.

In the short time we coached together, Soul touched many lives and endeared himself to the hearts of our players, and most of our community. Maybe it was the football memories generated by looking at the field I now stood on. Or maybe it was just the time of year; August, just before the season started.

Whatever it was, I missed my friend, Soul, more in moments like these than at just about any other time I could think of.

CHAPTER 2

"See ya, Milo!" Jamie called out, as Milo began walking down the street toward his home later that morning.

Both boys were hot and tired, but Milo managed to gather his energy as he turned around one more time.

"MUSTANG PRIDE!!!" Milo almost yelled as he pumped both of his fists in the air.

I smiled. "You sure you don't need a lift?"

Milo shook his head with conviction. "Walking," he said. "Helps me stay in shape. I'm gonna run the ball for Yearwood someday."

"I know you will," I grinned at him.

Milo's house, which he shared with his grandmother, was close to our campus and was within walking distance. So, Jamie and I stood together and watched as Milo headed toward his home, both of us smiling at the unique gait that we knew would always help define him. Milo's posture was always upright, and he always seemed to walk in a straight line no matter which direction he may have been heading. And yet, for all the straightness that characterized the rest of his body, his arms had a tendency to flail—or flap like wings—when he walked.

We sometimes called him "Bird" as a nickname, and Milo—in true Milo fashion—had taken it in stride and joked right along with us.

"Love that dude," I said to Jamie.

"He makes me laugh," Jamie agreed.

"Is that why you're friends with him?"

Jamie shook his head. "Not the whole reason. He keeps me humble, too."

I nodded, thinking I understood. "Helps you to not get too big-headed, especially as an athlete."

"Sort of," Jamie affirmed. "I was thinking more along the lines of just keeping life in perspective."

I glanced at him.

"Sports are cool," Jamie continued, "but life isn't guaranteed."

I patted my son on the shoulder, at a loss myself for what to say to him.

A day later, I received a text as I was walking out of our team's locker room, headed to the practice field behind our stadium.

It was from Jamie.

"Got the starting job!"

I pumped my fist and had to restrain myself from jumping into the air as I jogged out to the field.

There had always been little doubt in my mind that Jamie would start at quarterback for a high school team at some point. But ninth grade? Over an eleventh-grader?

My exhilaration soon gave way to a small amount of disappointment. Jamie's starting at quarterback on varsity meant that I likely would miss his Friday night games on weeks when Yearwood State had their away games. And there were five of those scheduled during the upcoming season.

I had known this day would come, but had figured that, in the early going, I could at least see him play all of his junior varsity games on Thursday nights. Even on weeks when I would have to leave on the road the next day, I'd still be around to cheer him on during those early years of high school. Now, it seemed that Jamie would likely never even play JV.

I shook off the negativity and decided to be happy that my only son was going to start at quarterback like his old man; and probably do a better job also. Jamie had inherited his height genes from his mother's biological father, a man who had given little else to his family. With this trait, combined with my expertise playing—and coaching—the position, Jamie was likely to go even farther in the game than I ever had.

"What are you so giddy about?" Jeff Swicegood asked as I walked up. "You look like the dumb kid in class who just made the honor roll."

I chuckled at my head coach as we stood together and watched our team captains lead warm-ups and stretching before practice began in earnest.

"Jamie got it," I told him. "Gonna start for Coach Richroath as a freshman."

Swicegood nodded his approval. "I'm not surprised," he said. "I've seen him play. Paul Hammond's got good tools, but Jamie's a natural; mature for his age, too."

I could not disagree.

"Only thing holding Jamie back," Swicegood went on, "is having a shitty former YSU quarterback for a dad. You sure he's got the right genes for this job?"

"Play reflects coaching," I shot back, with a wry grin. "Or is your old geezer memory so far gone that you've forgotten that?"

Both of us laughed. Jeff Swicegood had recruited me out of high school in 1998 when he was Yearwood State's offensive coordinator. Upon my arrival, he and I had spent countless hours during my college years practicing and breaking down game film. He had been an excellent mentor and coordinator who, several years later, had been promoted to head coach at YSU. By that time, I was coaching in my first season at Sims County High School in Florida, and Swicegood had offered me a job right after taking over as head coach. The timing was not right, though, and I had turned down his offer.

Moving and chasing the "next better job" is a part of coaching, and likely always will be. I suppose that's why some folks ridiculed my decision to stay in at my current job and not head back to the college ranks after one year of high school coaching. Still, Jeff Swicegood and I had maintained a close friendship in spite of that. I stayed at Sims County for six years, leaving after the 2009 season to coach at larger high schools across the southeast for the next seven years.

Finally, in 2017, Swicegood (who, after this season, would tie the record for longest coaching tenure at YSU) was able to lure me back to my collegiate alma mater as his offensive coordinator. And I'm glad he did, as the two of us have continued to work well together.

My offenses at YSU were not unique—a blend of finesse passing attack and bruising ground game, depending on our personnel. But they were always efficient and grounded in solid fundamentals. Swicegood loved them because they were a perfect fit for his blue-collar approach to the game.

"Tell you one thing," Swicegood said to me after a moment, as we watched the players break up into position drills, "I'll bet Richroath won't get anywhere near the pushback for his decision to start Jamie as a freshman than what we've gotten from you-know-who."

I chuckled, knowing that he had a point.

"Any more nasty-grams from Charlie Stinson?" I asked.

"No, but he did call and bitch at my secretary earlier this week," Swicegood replied. "Poor woman has a hard enough time working for me, she shouldn't have to listen to his egotistical mouth, too."

"Why'd he call?" I asked.

"Why do you think?" Swicegood said, looking at me for the first time from behind his Ray-Bans. He was far from the young, spry coordinator that had recruited me to Yearwood over a decade-and-a-half ago, but at nearly the age of fifty, Jeff Swicegood still harbored the same "coach's intensity" that he'd always had.

"I guess," he went on, "Stinson figures that if he badgers me enough, I'm going to finally give in and start his nephew at quarterback over Jakobe. But it doesn't work that way."

"Does he think that your secretary controls whether or not you're going to start Connor under center this Fall?" I followed up.

"I don't know what that jackass thinks half the time," Swicegood answered. "The Stinsons have been in the booster picture for Yearwood State for years, and ever since I voted—as the tie-breaking vote against renaming our field after his grandfather—he's been pissed at me. So, I guess that's part of it. And I guess he's also mad because of the direction our quarterback situation is going now. One thing's for sure, though, as long as he controls the damn purse strings of the program, Howser's going to let him talk to me however he pleases."

I winced. "It definitely sucks when the athletic director doesn't have your back against rich boosters," I told him, remembering some of the problems from my own days as head coach at Sims County.

"Yep."

We stood there for a moment, watching our defensive guys run two-on-two drills.

"Well," Swicegood said, "let's see if Connor can beat out Jakobe today, so I don't have to listen to Charlie bitch all season."

"Not likely," I replied with a laugh.

❧

"Settttt...Hut!"

Jakobe Ackerman took the snap, dashed out of the pocket on a designed roll-out, and executed a perfect throw downfield to Deon Flowers, one of our top receivers. Following that one, he had seven or eight others just like it.

I stood on the field behind where the play was happening, surveyed everything, and tried to remember the last time I had seen a quarterback with as much talent as Jakobe Ackerman. At six feet, two inches tall, and just over two-hundred and twenty pounds, he had a cannon for an arm and could run and create plays with his feet when an offensive scheme broke down. We were even drawing up option plays—something unheard of since I had taken over as offensive coordinator—now that he was on campus. He had transferred from the University of Louisville earlier in the year and would play as a junior.

His arrival, however –welcomed as it was by us coaches—had definitely complicated things.

Swicegood had for three years now been grooming Connor Judd, also a junior, to take over at quarterback this season—largely at the behest of Charlie Stinson, Connor's uncle and one of our wealthiest supporters of the program. Connor was a talented athlete but was playing at nowhere near the same level as Jakobe. But his work ethic was by far the biggest thing he had going for him. Everything was "yes sir," "no sir," and always went the extra mile on whatever he was asked to do.

Despite all this, it was becoming clearer by the day that he simply could not hang with Jakobe in terms of sheer talent.

And despite his uncle being a pain in the ass (however rich and generous a pain in the ass he was), Connor was about as different from him as you could ask for; down-to-earth and humble as they come in a kid his age.

Jakobe, on the other hand, was easygoing enough but definitely had a cocky streak about him.

Both were solid quarterbacks whom Swicegood and I were going to have to decide between prior to our first game against Marquis State at the end of the month. And as things stood right then, Jakobe had the clear edge.

"Blue team!" I called out. "Take water. Gold team, you're up!"

Jakobe led his offensive squad off of the field and in the direction of the water station, which was being supervised by Katie Corvin, a young sophomore co-ed who was majoring in sports science at YSU. Even though Jakobe trailed behind some of his teammates, Katie held out the first cup of water for him to take.

I chuckled to myself. "Katie's got a type, I guess," I said to Swicegood, who stood near me.

He just shook his head and smiled as Connor Judd got the Gold offense set up and ready for the first play.

I watched as Connor executed all ten plays well enough, though not with quite the same crispness that Jakobe had run them. Looking over at Swicegood, it was clear that selecting Connor as our starter might require an explanation; whereas Jakobe was using his skills on the field to explain himself.

One thing was for certain: whichever passer did get the job would be called upon to lead what was probably going to be one of our most talented rosters in recent memory.

Running the ball, we had "Downtown" Mathias Brown, a junior running back, who had rushed for over eight-hundred yards the season before. He was a dependable, proven ball-carrier, who would provide balance to our offense with a solid ground attack. He couldn't carry the team, but then again, he didn't need to. Like Jakobe, he also had a big personality, which meshed well with everyone and helped us stay loose and keep things fun.

Both our offensive and defensive lines were solid; with Clay Moss, our senior center, and Cam Grigsby, our left tackle anchoring things. On defense, Russell Villemont and Del McClelland were our two ends who could patrol the edge and pursue quarterbacks like it was easy. Reggie Arnold was our nose guard who stopped the run inside.

At linebacker, Adalius Bennett was a sophomore athletic freak who had the rare combination of size and speed that allowed our defensive coaches to line him up either at end or outside linebacker. Corey Nixon and Clint Gaines were our other two linebackers. Both were seniors and dependable leaders.

In the secondary, our defensive backs had the ability to knock away passes and shut down anybody going across the middle or downfield. It all started with Chris Whiteside and JaMond Matthews at corner, and Antonio Cannon and Pat Ripley at the two safety positions.

We were loaded on defense.

Even our kicking game was solid. Joey Cleverland was a solid punter who could help us flip our field position when the offense stalled, and Mike Carrow was a dependable placekicker who we knew we could rely on from anywhere inside the thirty-five-yard line.

"Let's call it a day," Swicegood told me two hours later.

"SOUL SPRINTS!" I called out.

Fifteen minutes later, after the grueling combination of calisthenics - push-ups, leg-lifts, burpees, and other miscellaneous exercises—followed by stadium step runs, the guys were kneeling or standing in a circle around our coaching staff and panting heavily. It was the same series of exercises and running that Jamie and I had done all summer, and it did wonders for our team's physical conditioning.

Soul Sprints—named after my college teammate, who had invented them himself—were another thing that always brought to mind memories of Soul Rasheed.

As Katie handed out cups of water to the players, Swicegood stood before them ready to speak.

"Guys," he began, "it's about execution, and it's about family; same thing you all have been hearing about from us since day one. Our execution still needs work in some areas; I'm seeing some missed tackles, missed blocks, missing fundamentals, and the like."

He paused.

"But one thing," he continued, holding up an index finger, "one thing I've noticed about you all, and what I've been real proud of, is the family aspect of things. You guys have stuck together all through the pre-season, going all the way back to spring practice, and then two-a-days earlier this summer. And you've done it in the middle of what's been some hard decision-making between myself and the coaches regarding a few of the positions…mainly quarterback."

I looked up and tried to conceal my surprise. It was unlike Jeff Swicegood to be that specific when it came to a topic as sensitive as position battles. The fact that he had mentioned the quarterback spot by name seemed to only add a degree of significance to the struggle for first-team.

As for the team, they just gave each other knowing glances. With or without Swicegood saying it, they knew. They knew that they would have a solid quarterback going into the season; the only question was "Which one?".

"And so I'm proud of you guys," Swicegood went on. "I'm proud of our team's effort; again, not just on the field, but in the locker room and when we take these pads off at the end of the day. Let's stay united, and let's finish strong so that we can kick some Marquis State ass come late August."

Rumblings of "Yeah!" and "Let's go!" and "Let's get it!" rippled throughout the group.

I glanced over at where Connor and Jakobe were standing. Both of them looked at each other and, as if to confirm what their head coach was saying, gave each other a friendly fist bump.

"Congrats, Coach!" Katie called to me, as we jogged off the practice field. She ambled up to me, her wavy blonde hair bouncing in the breeze, and smiled, showing a set of perfect white teeth. Katie Corvin had never been a cheerleader, but she could pass for one, and I had even heard her referred to before as our team's unofficial cheering section.

"Congrats for what?" I asked her, as I carried a sack full of equipment. "For being relegated to your job? Here," I said, thrusting the sack in her direction. "Take this."

"Sure," she said.

"I'm kidding," I told her. "I got this. Seriously, though, why are you congratulating me."

"For Jamie!" she exclaimed as if I should have known. "He got the starting job at the high school."

"How'd you know about that?" I asked, surprised.

Katie gave me a mock scowl. "Coach, when is it going to sink in for you that I'm the daughter you never had? Your wife and I are close; we text practically every day."

I chuckled because it was true. Dixie had met Katie shortly after she had joined up with the team, and the two had hit it off.

They often went out to lunch between semesters, when Katie wasn't in her hometown in Ohio. Katie had even spent Christmas with us the season before.

"So, when's the wedding?" I asked her, moments later.

"What wedding?"

"Between you and Jakobe," I said, cutting my eyes at her playfully.

She punched me in the arm. "You know we're just friends."

"Figured it was more than that from the way you gave him that first cup of water earlier; never mind the fact that he wasn't even first in line."

"He's the quarterback," she protested. "It's a big job."

"Some would say a bigger job is keeping Jakobe off his ass," I replied with a grin. "Clay Moss would make that argument. How come he didn't get that first cup?"

Katie just rolled her eyes and shook her head.

"You know I'm needling you," I said, elbowing her. "Heck, you're the reason Jakobe's done so well in school this semester; his first one, no less."

"He's a sweet guy," she said. "And it's been fun to tutor and help him out. Plus, I know he's been through a lot."

"The accusation," I said, almost to myself.

I heard Jakobe speak up as he walked behind me. "Accusation, nothing," he said with a good-natured grin. "Fresh start, Coach Leonard. You know this."

I turned and nodded to him. "It sure is."

"All that stuff's in the past," Jakobe added, coming between Katie and me, and staring off in the distance.

"Well, from the way your grades are improving," Katie told him, as they walked side by side, "I'd say the future looks pretty bright."

Jakobe smiled at her as they continued walking. "Thanks."

Jakobe and I parted ways with Katie at the locker room entrance, and I handed the equipment to her for unpacking in a nearby closet. Jakobe hugged her as he went inside the locker room to change.

"You coming tonight?" I asked her before following Jakobe inside.

"Where?"

I gave her an incredulous stare. "You mean Dixie didn't tell you?"

"To celebrate at Tootsie's?"

"Yeah," I said with a laugh. "We've been planning it for weeks, saying that if Jamie got the starting nod at quarterback we'd go out to dinner…"

"…and have a big surprise," she said, her eyes lighting up. "Of course, I know about that."

"Do you know about the surprise?"

"Coach," she frowned, "again, I'm the daughter you never had."

"So we'll see you there tonight?"

"Tootsie's Bar and Grill. I'll be there."

CHAPTER 3

By that evening, I had lost count of how many times I had checked my phone throughout the day. Between texts from my wife and Deke Hudson, our close family friend, I felt as though my face had been glued to my touch-screen since waking up that morning.

Dixie and I had been married for fifteen years, but lately, it felt as though we were mere roommates who happened to share a kid and a home; always on the go, and usually preoccupied with all things sports; either Jamie's or mine, or both.

Tootsie's Grill and Bar was the location of choice that evening for our mini-celebration of Jamie's winning the starting quarterback spot. As I got out of the car, I glanced at the aging building, which Bud and Winnifred Pearlmuter had owned for decades; since well before I had come to Yearwood as an eighteen-year-old scholarship player from rural Florida.

The small, locally-owned restaurant had been a mainstay in Yearwood for as long as most people in the town could remember.

I went in and was immediately greeted by a familiar face.

"What's up, boy!" Max Tankersley said to me. "Got your table ready. Katie's already here."

I smiled at him and said, "Great."

Max Tankersley and his identical twin, Woody, had been known as the "Twin Tanks" back in college. They had become my friends during my second season as a player in Yearwood and were from Fort Wayne, Indiana. Both were offensive linemen who had blocked for me, and both were as dependable and capable a pair of blockers as a quarterback could ask for. After graduation, they—along with Soul—had come with me from Yearwood to Lake Barrow and had helped me make memories on the sidelines at Sims County as assistant coaches.

Max now worked at Tootsie's as a general manager.

"Did you text Deke?" Max asked me.

I smiled, thinking of the elaborate plan that was coming together for my son's celebration.

"All day long."

"Can't wait to see Jamie's face," Max grinned.

"How's business?" I asked him.

"Tolerable," he answered, as he wiped a thin layer of sweat from his bald forehead. "Gets busy during the season."

In college, Max and Woody had been almost indistinguishable. Both were heavyset with ruddy complexions and red hair. Through the years, though, Max had gone bald, eventually choosing to shave all of his hair off; while Woody—at least in recent pictures that I had seen—still had a full head.

"How's Mama Freddy today?" I asked.

"She's good," Max said. "She'll be here in a few minutes."

"Seriously?"

"Oh yeah," Max nodded. "As soon as I mentioned that Deke Hudson was going to give Jamie a shout-out live on Sports News, she was all in. *'Ain't missing it for the world!'*" Max delivered this last line in a high-pitched mimicry of the woman who had fed us countless meals throughout our college years.

Winnifred "Mama Freddy" Pearlmuter, along with her husband, Bud, were not only the founders of Tootsie's Bar and Grill but were also lifelong boosters to the Yearwood State football program, members of just about every civic organization that Yearwood had to offer, and were the parents that many college kids—football players especially—never had.

In college, I had spent countless hours at their house, especially during football season, where homecooked meals were always in abundance, as well as a place to stay when holiday travel home was not possible. In the off-season, Bud had also hired me to work at his restaurant.

"Ever think about getting back into coaching?" I asked Max.

Max shook his head. "This is home," he said. "And Mama Freddy needs me."

Max had a point. After Bud had died years earlier and left behind to Mama Freddy what little he had—including the restaurant—she had hired Max and turned nearly all day-to-day operations over to him.

Max studied me. "Just you, the family, and Katie tonight?"

I shook my head. "They're bringing Milo with them."

"I love that kid," Max smiled as he continued wiping down menus. "I think what impresses me the most about Jamie's relationship with him is that you can tell he's not doing it as a charity thing. He genuinely cares about Milo and wants to be his friend."

I nodded and agreed. "They've been best friends since we moved here back in '17."

"I'm not surprised," Max said. "Seems like every time you all come in here, Milo's tagging right along with you."

"Yeah," I said with a smile. "How's Woody doing?"

Max shook his head. "He's Woody."

"Still living in Fort Wayne?"

"Still in Fort Wayne, still living with our parents off and on." I shook my head.

"Can't figure out what he wants to do when he grows up. Tried to move his girlfriend in with my parents; they said no;

Woody almost got kicked out. Last I heard, he was working odd jobs and trying to get some vague degree through one of those for-profit schools."

"What's his college degree in? Sports management."

Max nodded.

"So why not go back into coaching?"

"Lazy," Max said. "You know I love my brother, but he needs to fix himself."

My mind went back to the time we spent coaching together in Sims County. After that fateful first season, when Soul had been killed, the Twin Tanks had stayed with me for two more years, Max coaching offensive line, and Woody coaching defense. After that, they had gone their separate ways, never to coach again. For me, this was sad, since both of them were more than capable as line coaches. Max ended up back in Yearwood and had not left since, while Woody had roamed nonstop after leaving Lake Barrow. As brothers, Woody and Max Tankersley were close, but I often marveled at how different they were from each other, even as twins.

"Your brood's here," Max said, gesturing toward the door.

I glanced behind me and, sure enough, Dixie entered, followed by Jamie, who towered above her, and Milo who walked beside him. Both boys were engaged in a rapturous conversation to which Dixie was oblivious or was trying to be.

"Hey, Max!" she greeted him with a hug, before turning to me and saying "Hey, you," with a kiss.

Fifteen years of marriage and her kisses still rocked my world. She was wearing a sleeveless shirt with the tail tucked in, blue jeans, and her blonde hair pulled back into a bun. Her radiant green eyes sparkled, just as they always had, and brought a singular light to her face that had always attracted me. She had a curvaceous figure, something I had always liked about her, and she had worn the weight well, even after having Jamie years ago.

Max showed us to our booth and handed out menus, as we all greeted Katie and sat down.

"What are we drinking, champion?" Max asked Jamie. "Beer, champagne?"

"I'd like a beer," Jamie said.

"Stop that," Dixie shushed, with a playful grin.

"Uncle Max is a bad influence," Max self-deprecated. "Don't listen to me. Seriously, though, what's your poison?"

"I'll take a root beer," Jamie said.

"Done deal," Max affirmed. Then, turning to Milo, he asked, "How about you, Bird?"

"Root beer," Milo echoed Jamie, his bright face smiling up at Max.

Max disappeared after Dixie and I both ordered water and Katie a soft drink.

Katie then leaned over in my direction. "I have a few extra bucks tonight, Coach, if you want me to cover my own."

I brushed her off without a thought. "We're paying," I insisted.

"Are you sure?" Katie asked, without much conviction.

"Positive," I said and noticed the subtle relief that came to her face and shoulders as I settled it. "Send that extra money home to your parents."

"Thanks," Katie said quietly with a grateful smile.

"How are they doing?" I asked.

"Good," Katie answered. "I mean, physically, they're both doing fine. Dad's PT is going well, and Mom seems to be responding okay to the new heart medication from the doctor."

"That's good to hear."

"Financially…" she continued, before trailing off.

I reached over and patted her arm. "You don't have to say anything," I comforted. "Are you going to be able to stay in Yearwood?"

Katie looked up at me with the same vivacious eyes, but there was a hollowness in her look. "I'm good for this semester," she told me. "After that, we'll see."

On a personal level, my heart often felt that it was breaking whenever the subject of Katie Corvin's finances came up. During her senior year of high school, both of her parents had come into severe physical issues that had nearly bankrupted her family. Katie's student loans were helping with tuition, but she had little else to draw from, money-wise. She was a smart girl and a good student who enjoyed life at Yearwood State, and yet it seemed as though the possibility of her having to drop out and go home to Ohio to help care for her parents was always on the horizon.

For me, it was heartbreaking because my journey to Yearwood State years earlier had almost mirrored the one she was on now.

"Did y'all come straight from practice?" I asked, changing the subject as I wrinkled my nose.

"Yeah," Dixie said. "Why?"

Katie jumped in. "'Cause you can smell Jamie all the way out in the parking lot."

Milo burst out laughing. Jamie gave a playful grin, wadded up a piece of napkin, and threw it at her. She was every bit the "big sister" to him as she was a daughter to us.

"Or maybe it's Milo," I added, causing Milo's face to register shock and mock disgust.

"Or maybe it's you because you're not ready for the big game!" Katie exclaimed.

I grinned, as the back-and-forth banter continued.

It was a no-brainer that Milo had become the second son we'd never had, just like Katie had been unofficially adopted as a daughter to us. I suppose that, in a way, these were God's ways of giving us what our family needed, whether we knew it or not. Several years after Jamie had been born, we tried to have a second child, but it was to no avail. Fertility treatments proved unfruitful, and while the idea of adoption had crossed our minds, it had never become an earnest pursuit. From there, life had gotten in the way, and we soon resolved to just be happy with Jamie and the other "kids" we were blessed to come in contact with.

Still, as I watched Katie banter back and forth with Dixie about all things girl-related, my heart warmed as I pictured what having a daughter may have looked like for us. Dixie loved spending time with Katie and ate up every opportunity that she had to talk with her.

I looked at my son across the table from me as he cut up with Milo, and smiled. With or without the athletic ability, Jamie was a compassionate, kind-hearted, hard-working kid who put his mind and heart into whatever he did; personally or when it came to a task.

He was over six feet tall now and, while lanky, had the unmistakable frame of someone who would one day put on muscle weight if he kept working out. As I watched him at the table that evening, he reminded me of Dixie in his mannerisms and interactions with Katie and Milo. And I found myself wondering just how far back I could trace—beyond Dixie—where it all came from. It was a bittersweet thought; sweet in the sense that I knew it came from Dixie's side of the family, but bitter in that some of it may have come from her biological father, whom she never knew.

For my part, it was the same story. As I look at it, maybe not being able to see your father in your kids is just one more cross to bear when you come from a single-parent home. Maybe that's part of our "soul sprint" in life, as I like to call it.

"So," Dixie said, snapping me out of my reverie. "Any news on your quarterback front?"

I sighed, leaned back in the booth, and rubbed my eyes. Just thinking about our quarterback controversy was enough to make the nerves in my head start tensing and hurting

"In all honesty, it's probably Jakobe's to lose," I answered. "Swicegood wants it to be Connor, though."

Dixie frowned, which deepened the lines in her near-middle-aged face. "Charlie Stinson sure does, we know that."

I rolled my eyes. "Charlie's Charlie."

"He still raising cane at Jeff?"

"Charlie's going to raise cane at everyone, so long as Quinn Howser lets him do it," I replied.

Dixie gave another frown and then reached over for my hand. "You and Jeff will make the right decision," she affirmed. "You always do."

Twenty minutes later, Max brought out our pizza, and we dug in.

"Mama Freddy's on her way up here," he told me as he began walking away. "She just texted me."

"She *texts* now?" I asked.

"Oh yeah," Max said. "Had to spend about a half hour showing her how to do it, but yeah, the old gal can text."

I laughed. "Can't wait to see her."

"She's excited to see you, too," Max winked at me as he walked away.

"So," I said, turning back to the table, as plates were filled with slices, "what's a goal you guys have for this year?"

Jamie gave a light-hearted roll of the eyes. "Here we go," I heard him mutter.

"What?" I asked. "You know it's something we talk about at the start of each school year...not to mention, each football season."

"Throw for a bunch of yards."

"Measurable," I repeated.

Jamie thought for a moment. "Win a state championship."

I gave him a surprised look. "Swinging for the fences," I said.

Jamie shrugged. "Maybe, but if not this year, then definitely at some point."

"What about this year?" I asked him. "Any short-term goals."

Jamie thought for a moment. Then he cast glances in both mine and Dixie's directions and said with conviction, "That's the goal. I want a state ring."

"Ok," I said, after nodding at Dixie, who signaled her agreement. "Go for it. And how about you, Milo?"

Milo sat chewing on a slice of pepperoni pizza, his mouth stained with sauce, as he pondered the question.

"I want to run for a touchdown," he finally said.

I smiled at him, though in the back of my mind, I was trying to think of a gentle way to steer him in a different direction. He had never played sports, nor would he likely ever, due to his myriad medical conditions.

Jamie must have picked up on my concealed skepticism, because he said, "Milo could do it."

"Of course, he can," Dixie blurted quickly.

I wanted to chime in about something more realistic, but Dixie gave me a subtle, yet unmistakable look, and the issue was settled.

It was settled in the same rapid-fire, decisive way that Dixie decided most things when it came to Milo...or Jamie...or really, just about any kid; especially if the kid in question was in a difficult spot. She never said it out loud, but it was always evident in those deep, green, passionate eyes of hers that it wasn't just Milo she was caring for, it was a reflection of herself. Dixie had known instability and poverty as a child more than most kids ever would.

"Sounds good," I agreed. "I hope you get to score that touchdown."

For the first time, Milo took a break from his pizza frenzy, looked up at me, and grinned a pizza-sauce-stained grin.

"Mustang pride!" he beamed, giving me a thumbs-up.

"How are my kids doing?" Mama Freddy asked as she hobbled toward our table with a cane moments later.

I rose and gave her frail body a gentle hug, which she returned.

Winnifred Pearlmuter had once been a robust woman—not too hefty, but not petite either. And yet, her age and declining health had taken their toll. Still, she approached us with the same beaming grin that I had always been greeted with upon arrival at her and Bud's house. Her grin was a way, at least for me, of saying, "Welcome home," somehow. And I always loved her for it.

"How are you, Mama?" I asked her.

"Gettin' along fine," she answered, before quickly turning to Dixie, Katie, and the boys. Everyone exchanged hugs with her, including Milo.

We pulled a chair up to our table, and Mama Freddy sat in it, facing the rest of us as we occupied the booth.

"How's the pizza?" she asked the boys.

"Awesome," Jamie said.

Milo was still working on his and gave her a messy thumbs-up.

Dixie and Katie made small talk with Mama Freddy for a few moments, while I periodically checked my phone, waiting to hear from Deke about Jamie's big TV surprise.

Soon, Mama Freddy turned to me. "How's the team looking, Coach?" she asked.

"Good," I said. "Still deciding on a quarterback."

For the first time since she had come to our table that evening, Mama Freddy frowned. "Makes me so sick! It needs to be Jakobe, but that damned Charlie Stinson just can't keep his hands out of things, and isn't going to stop until Connor starts, no matter what."

I nodded and couldn't help but smile.

"That's why I don't go to Mustang booster meetings anymore," she went on. "Of course, part of it's also because Bud's no longer here to go with me, and it just isn't the same without him. But the Stinsons have been insufferable to work with ever since that power play Charlie made to become chairman of the boosters. And I just can't stomach those phony get-togethers anymore."

I had to stifle a laugh, even though she was serious. Mama Freddy was pushing eighty now but was not lacking in energy or spunk.

"Things will work out," I said, reaching over and patting her hand.

"You've always had so much hope, Jayce," she responded, the grin returning to her face. "Even when things weren't so good, you kept everyone's spirits up."

"I had two good adoptive parents here at Yearwood to help me with that," I said to her.

Mama Freddy squeezed my hand.

At that moment, my cell phone buzzed. I checked it; sure enough, it was another text message from Deke Hudson.

Shout-out in five; change the channel now!

I quickly shot a text over to Max and told him to *change all the channels.*

Within a couple of minutes, every television—including the one broadcasting the preseason game that Jamie and Milo were watching – was on Sports News.

"What happened to the game?" Jamie asked a mild outrage creasing across his face. Milo just sat and stared at the television blankly, as if he too was wondering.

"Just watch," I told them both, trying to conceal my excitement.

The announcer, an older man, then said: *We now pause our regularly scheduled broadcast and will cut over to our main studio, where Deke Hudson has an important announcement.*

"Uncle Deke!" Jamie and Milo exclaimed in unison when Deke Hudson appeared on screen.

I sat and smiled as I watched my former high school teammate on screen; the same one who had gone on to break rushing records at the University of Florida as a running back, and then gone on to enjoy an illustrious career as a Tampa Bay Buccaneer. Despite being an all-world pro, who was now retired and working as a broadcaster at Sports News, Deke Hudson had remained close with me through some of the most dramatic ups and downs of my life. He had become a close friend when I had first moved to Lake Barrow as a youngster. He had been there when Rex, my stepfather, had been killed during my elementary school days. He had been there during high school, as we made memories playing together on the football field, and he had been there through the death of two of my closest friends; Jamie Gill and Soul Rasheed.

And now, he was about to surprise the heck out of my only son.

Dixie had her phone out and was trying to be discreet as she started videoing Jamie as he and Milo watched the screen.

I just sat next to Mama Freddy, both of us with wry grins on our faces.

Yeah, thanks Chuck, Deke said, his hulking frame taking up most of the screen. *You know, in this crazy sports world of ours, it's not every day we get to connect with those friends who are closest to us; either from back home, or just those we've met along the way. And that's why it's important to pause every once in a while and give a shout-out to those of our closest loved ones who deserve it the most. And that's what I want to do tonight. This evening, I want to give a special shout-out to a very special someone who just earned the starting quarterback job as a ninth-grader on his football team.*

Deke paused for dramatic effect and then continued.

Jamie Leonard, of Yearwood High School in Yearwood, Kentucky—his dad and I played a little ball together—I'm proud of you, boy. You're gonna do great things! Keep going strong, and remember: tested and tried, Spartan pride!

I remember Jamie being born. I remember his first steps; his first words; and the first time he set foot both on a Pop Warner football field and a baseball diamond.

But as I sat there in that restaurant booth, watching his eyes go wide and his mouth go agape with disbelief as he listened to the legendary Deke Hudson say his name on national television—with Milo shrieking for joy, and Mama Freddy and Katie and Dixie beaming with laughter and pride—I knew it was a sight that almost none of those things could ever rival.

It was a great night.

CHAPTER 4

"The same way I enjoy a prostate exam," Jeff Swicegood groused, after I asked him whether or not he enjoyed "these booster dinners."

I cackled out loud at his response as the two of us, decked out in sport coats and ties, entered the Yearwood Country Club Event Hall several evenings later.

"Getting dressed up is one thing," he grumbled as he fought with his tie. "Having a constant reminder that Charlie Stinson thinks we're his ball-washers is another."

"Let's just get through it," I told him.

The two of us signed in at a small folding table in the lobby, which was draped with a banner that read, "Yearwood State University Athletic Boosters."

Swicegood, as the head coach, was immediately swarmed as we entered the large and ornate dining room. I stuck nearby and shook a few hands, but was impressed at how he worked the room and was friendly, even though he did not want to be there.

Soon, we made our way to our seats in the large room.

The event hall was set up with round tables which were spaced throughout, and two lines of long, rectangular tables conjoined near the far wall with a podium separating them at the center. It was the VIP table, where we would be sitting.

Two placards with our names marked our seats, and both of us smiled as we realized that we'd be sitting on either flank of Denvis McBride.

"Thank God," Swicegood said.

"I think Charlie's on the other side of the podium from us," I added.

"Like I said, 'thank God'."

On cue, we heard a deep, booming voice behind us. "Coaches, it's great to see you this fine evening."

We turned and, sure enough, were greeted by the vice president of the Yearwood State Booster Club, Denvis McBride.

Denvis had played defensive end for the Mustangs back in the '90s and was now an ordained minister and pastor of a small AME church in Yearwood. In addition, he also served as president of the largest bank in town. He had graduated with a degree in finance and had then proceeded to gradually work his way up through the ranks in the worlds of both finance and YSU boosters. His success story was one of the most cherished among the alumni of our college. Everyone who knew Denvis McBride loved him.

He beamed at us and grasped our hands with his massive one as we shook.

"Good to see you, Den," Swicegood affirmed.

"You as well," he said, with a wide grin. "And how are you, Coach Leonard? Keeping my friend, Jeff, here, out of trouble?"

"C'mon, Den," I said with a playful smile. "I don't get paid enough for that job."

Denvis replied with a booming laugh, and said, "So is that your way of asking for a raise?"

"Maybe so."

"Darth Vader here yet?" Swicegood asked, scanning the room.

"I haven't seen him," Denvis said. "He normally waits till the last minute to show up. You know how he is."

"We all know," Swicegood replied.

"Gotta remind people that he doesn't work for them," Denvis added.

Swicegood nodded. "Step two is him realizing that we don't work for him either."

"This is true," Denvis agreed with a grin.

"I'm gonna get lost in the crowd," Swicegood told us, "before Stinson arrives."

With that, Swicegood rose from his seat and started making another pass through the event hall.

In truth, no one knew better than Denvis McBride the tribulations of working with a guy like Charlie Stinson, YSU's Booster Club president. Swicegood and I had often marveled at Denvis's dedication to the program, since serving as vice president of the Boosters meant working with Charlie on a regular basis.

"Mama Freddy says 'hello'." I told him, eager to change the subject.

Denvis lit up again. "Man, I haven't seen her in ages!" he exclaimed. "How is she doing?'

"Getting along well," I responded. "Saw her at Tootsie's the other night, when we were out celebrating Jamie. You know he won the starting quarterback job, right?"

"I heard about that," Denvis said with a proud smile. "So happy to hear it."

I thanked him and said, "So are we."

"That gangly kid," Denvis marveled, "that I met when we introduced you as offensive coordinator in this very room a few years ago is now going to start varsity as a freshman. Time definitely flies."

"It sure does."

"I'll have to come see some of his games."

"He'd love that," I said. "

"Is Mama Freddy still going to cook for the team this year?"

I shrugged. "The subject hasn't come up, but my guess would be that it'll be hard for her to do it this year. She's just not as able to do what she used to, especially now that Bud's gone."

Denvis frowned. "Gonna be the end of an era. I don't think I could even estimate how many meals I had at their house back when I was a player; much less know how many players they've fed for the last several decades. I do love me some Mama Freddy, and I hate she's no longer involved with the Boosters."

I nodded in agreement. "We know who to thank for that."

"I know, right?" Denvis said, rolling his eyes. "One could argue that Mama Freddy's cooking is what powered our team for so many years, especially during those years when we were really winning."

"I hear you," I told him. "Especially this year, since we're poised to do some serious winning again. It'd be a shame to see it fall apart just because Mama Freddy's not here to cook for us."

Denvis chuckled and nodded his head. "This is true. Although word on the street is that the quarterback situation might cause it to implode a whole lot quicker than the pre-game menu."

I grimaced.

"Charlie's worried," Denvis added.

"Charlie's worried that his nephew won't be the starter," I stated. "But it's not his decision."

"I get it," Denvis said, giving me a grin-and-bear-it look. "He's like a lot of rich guys; wants his way, and won't stop at anything to get it. And right now, he wants Connor in that starting role pretty badly."

"The same way," I rejoined, "that he wanted his late grandfather's name put on our stadium masthead, and got royally pissed when it didn't happen; no matter how many thousands of dollars such an operation would have cost us. And that was back during the lean years when budgets were tight."

"I know," Denvis said. "That's what really started the rift between him and Swicegood. Everyone, including Howser, was ready to vote for it. But Swicegood refused, breaking the unanimous vote that was needed to secure it, and keeping Charlie from getting his way. And brother, that's something that you don't want to do right there."

I chuckled. "So you're saying Jeff's in trouble for not kissing Charlie's ass?"

"Anything's possible," Denvis affirmed. "With Charlie Stinson, you never know."

Both of us were silent for a moment.

"Why do you stick around, Denvis?" I asked. "You could easily pour more of your time effort and energy into other areas, like your church. Why continue working with an insufferable prick like Charlie Stinson?"

Denvis thought for a moment, and then answered, "Same reason you're still around, Coach Leonard." He then grinned that broad, trademark grin by which everyone knew Denvis McBride. "Mustang pride."

"I want to thank everyone for showing up tonight," Quinn Howser began minutes later. "And I especially want to thank the Yearwood State Boosters for hosting this magnificent event. They have worked hard and continue to work hard on behalf of our student-athletes and our university. I want to thank you all for coming, and I do not want to steal too much thunder from our Booster president."

He paused here and gestured with a smile in the direction of Charlie Stinson.

"Charlie's credentials and achievements speak for themselves, and one need only to take a cursory glance around our campus to understand that. Charlie, is there an athletic building on this campus that doesn't have your family's name on it?" he asked.

"Only the football stadium," Charlie retorted, causing the room to break out in laughter at the irony. Howser was visibly embarrassed, and Charlie shot a glare back at Swicegood, who returned fire.

Howser managed to gracefully end his remarks and take his seat moments later.

Charlie Stinson then took the dais and began speaking, his oily, southern brogue reverberating throughout the spacious hall.

He was a tall man in his late fifties and, by all accounts, was aging well. He stood at just over six feet, and had a lanky build, but carried himself in a manner that was both dignified and graceful; befitting a man of position and status. His thick, salt-and-pepper hair was always coiffed and combed with just the right amount of precision, and he greeted everyone with a warm, fatherly manner and smile.

He was from a long line of Kentucky wealth and privilege. The Stinsons owned a horse farm that had been in their family for generations, and theirs was a family that had seen multiple members succeed in careers ranging from finance to politics to law to business to horse racing, and far beyond all of those. Charlie Stinson, for his part, was a founding partner in one of the largest land development firms in the Ohio Valley region and the Midwest, in addition to being our Booster Club president.

"Tonight," he intoned, as he stood behind the dais, "we have much to celebrate, much to anticipate, and much to be thankful for as boosters. It is a great time to be a Yearwood State Mustang!"

Applause rose in a din and echoed throughout the building.

"We are very thankful for the efforts of not only our superb student-athletes at Yearwood State, but also of our coaches, and our administrators. They continue to make us all proud to be Yearwood State Mustangs and will, with our continued support, continue the winning traditions that have made Yearwood State a destination of choice for young athletes throughout the nation coming out of high school. Mr. Quinn Howser, our athletic director, and his coaches of the various sports, are a solid team, and we're thankful to have him as a partner as we journey forward and continue making YSU a great place to study, live, and excel on the field of play."

More applause.

I glanced over at Swicegood, who made a furtive "jerking off" motion with his hand under the table, careful to keep it out of the sight of everyone except me and Denvis, who was seated between us. I grinned and heard Denvis chuckle.

Charlie soon finished up his remarks. When he had sat down, the lights dimmed, and a projector beamed video images onto a large screen high up on the wall behind us. It was a promotional recording, touting YSU sports, and we watched as footage of the previous seasons for the different sports flashed onto the screen. Football, volleyball, swimming, baseball, softball, golf, and many others were represented. The video was accompanied by up-tempo rock music and narration by a paid commentator, who urged supporters to keep up their support by donating money to the athletic program.

When the video was over, Quinn Howser rose again. Our athletic director was a squat heavy, balding man who had won a scholarship as a walk-on basketball player many years ago, and had parlayed that success into a career as an athletic administrator.

"Again, I want to thank you all for being here," he began in a high-pitched tone. "I hope your dinner is good, though I've heard some rumblings about having this get-together here, as opposed to Mama Freddy Pearlmuter's house."

This drew loud laughter, as well as some applause and *whoops* of affirmation. I found myself marveling once more at Mama Freddy and Bud's impact on the college, as well as on the town of Yearwood, Kentucky.

"We do appreciate folks like the Pearlmuters," Howser continued, "and we appreciate all of you. Without the kind of support we enjoy, this athletic program and its accomplishments would not be possible."

He went on for several more minutes, before introducing Swicegood, who stood up, went to the dais, and began offering a few remarks about our football team. He spoke for about twenty minutes, about depth, positions, schedule, and other matters that were usually on the minds of the boosters during the preseason. When he had finished, he opened the floor for questions.

The dinner was for all sports, but like most athletic programs with a football team, our sport was king, so more time would be allotted to Swicegood both for talking and for fielding questions.

"Question in the back," Swicegood said, pointing toward the rear of the room, where an older gentleman stood up. A young intern from Howser's office had a portable microphone and dashed to where the man was standing, handing it to him.

"Yeah, Coach Swicegood," the man began, "I was just wondering about something that I'm sure is on everyone's mind. Can you comment on the so-called 'quarterback controversy' between Jakobe Ackerman and Connor Judd? Where do we stand with that, and is it fair to say that Jakobe Ackerman is being given preferential treatment because of his having transferred to Yearwood from a larger school?"

It was a loaded question, and we all knew it. The dais was far enough back from where we were sitting that I could see Charlie Stinson, seated on the other side of us. A look of smug, shit-eating satisfaction creased his face, as he glowered at our coach, who refused to acknowledge him, and instead looked at the questioner.

"We're not close to a decision yet," Swicegood answered in an abrupt tone of voice. "Both players are playing well, have played well, and we'll have to see which one comes out on top as the opening game gets closer."

Charlie Stinson's arrogant smirk gradually faded into a glare of contempt, as Swicegood continued taking questions.

"Son of a bitch ambushed me," Swicegood said, as we strode across the parking lot an hour later, eager to get home to our families. "And don't you think he didn't, either."

"I don't," I placated.

"He probably paid that jackass in the back of the room to ask that question."

"I mean, the question was bound to come out at some point," I stated, "regardless of who Stinson may or may not have put up to it."

"Give me a break," Swicegood answered with a sidelong scowl. "The fact that it was an expected question was just more smokescreen for him to pull some shit like that."

I almost replied but decided not to. Pressing Jeff Swicegood when he was pissed was a bad idea, a lesson I had learned early on as a Yearwood State player.

"Word is," Swicegood carried on, "Charlie Stinson never wanted a damn thing to do with that sister of his—Connor's mom—after she got pregnant out of wedlock, and then ran off and married the father—probably to spite the entire, wretched Stinson clan. Except now that Connor's a rising star on the football field, Stinson figures he can use Connor as leverage to get at me."

I just nodded.

"Yo, boys!"

We turned and saw Denvis McBride coming up behind us, his hulking frame hustling to keep pace with us.

"Y'all walk fast when you're upset, that's for sure," he said, smiling good-naturedly as he approached.

"What's up, Den?" I asked.

"Just wanted to try and smooth things over before the night was out," he said. "'Don't let the sun go down on your anger,' as the Bible says."

"I wish the sun would go down on Charlie Stinson's influence over our program," Swicegood replied.

I smiled at Denvis. "We're fine, Den. Just griping about Charlie."

"I hear you," Denvis agreed. "Listen, I just want you guys to know that you're doing a fine job. We're all proud of you, and happy with you."

"All?" Swicegood was skeptical.

"Don't worry about Stinson," Denvis assured. "Just focus on the team, and the rest will take care of itself."

CHAPTER 5

Swicegood ended practice early the next day.

The reason for this was our customary, annual visit from the Office of Student Safety and Advocacy (OSSA).

This particular office had been an obscure one on our campus for much of its existence. However, that had changed with the advent of the #MeToo movement, which had only recently become a hot topic on college campuses, ours included. Thanks to #MeToo, our OSSA was now finding itself with all the support it needed. Money, publicity, and time set aside for OSSA personnel to train clubs, fraternities, and sports teams, were now in abundance. No expense or resource was spared in order to keep Yearwood State from becoming a byword in mishandling sexual assault cases.

Darcy DeMarr, an intense, educated woman of almost fifty, was one such resource. She had been brought in by the university to oversee the newly formed Sexual Assault and Prevention Advocacy Program within the OSSA at Yearwood State. Up until recently, all handling of sexual assault cases had been farmed out to various existing personnel within OSSA, almost as a collateral duty. #MeToo had changed all of that, and Darcy now spent her days single-handedly training, lecturing, and overseeing the devastating cases of assault victims that crossed her desk.

Today, she had been scheduled by Quinn Howser to speak to our football team. While nobody within our football program was particularly looking forward to what she had to say, we all knew that what she had to say was vital just the same.

"The last several years have been difficult when it comes to this topic," she said, about midway into her speech. "And a lot of that has to do with the fact that sexual assault is preventable."

The players, for the most part, were listening to her. Darcy was a tallish woman with short, dark hair and an athletic build. Her stature, as well as her voice, commanded respect.

"Sexual assault is real," she went on, "and it involves sexual contact without…what?"

"Consent," a few players replied in unison.

"Consent," she affirmed. "That's right. The minute you do not have consent is the minute sexual activity needs to stop… otherwise, it's an assault. Period."

She paused to let her final words sink in.

"That's all I have, Coach," she said, turning to Swicegood.

"Thanks, Darcy," he said, taking his place in front of the team.

As Swicegood began speaking, Darcy walked over to me.

"Coach Leonard," she greeted me with a smile and a fist bump.

"Good to see you again," I told her.

Though Darcy had only been with the university a short time, she and I had crossed paths on several occasions and had hit it off well. Her father had been a football coach, and she had grown up in the shadow of many stadiums herself. We always had plenty to talk about.

"Thanks for having me out here," she added. "Love talking to the team, even though I'm sure the feeling isn't mutual. Pretty sure they'd rather be heading home than listening to me."

"Don't worry about that," I encouraged.

"Wouldn't give it to them if I didn't care about them. Too many athletes get into trouble with stuff like this. Breaks my heart. Always broke my dad's, too."

I nodded.

Swicegood was saying, "Guys, if you're uncertain about where I stand on this sexual assault issue, and where our coaches stand, all you gotta do is look back at the past couple of seasons. You all know about the guys we've let go from here because of their inability to treat others with respect, especially involving sex-related matters. It's zero tolerance around here. No exceptions. No questions asked."

I kept my eyes on our team. A few eyes darted in the direction of Jakobe Ackerman, a teammate whose history was well known, and who everybody knew was on a tight leash where this topic was concerned.

"Don't forget it," Swicegood ended.

Switching gears, I decided after practice to head in the direction of Jamie's school, where I knew he would be practicing with his teammates. It was something I seldom got to do, and I relished the opportunity.

I've always been a firm believer that the purest form of football is often found on the high school fields of play. It is on the high school field where the love of the game comes forth. The grass stains seem more real; the bond between communities and the team is more authentic, and kids just want to get out there and compete—even if some have visions of future grandeur, glory, and wealth in the back of their minds.

High school football is football at its purest. And not even my own negative experiences as a high school coach could erase that.

Jamie emerged from the locker room a half hour after practice had ended. I had watched him play, soaking up every snap he took, and watching him develop into the elite player that I knew he could one day be.

I watched and waited as my son came out wearing a pair of athletic shorts, and the t-shirt he'd worn under his pads, which was drenched with sweat. His blonde hair was tousled as he trudged forward, exhausted.

I nodded to him, and he gave me a faint grin; glad to see me, but determined to not be "uncool" by showing it.

"Hey, champ," I said.

"Hey," he almost whispered.

"Rough practice?"

Jamie shrugged. "It's all right."

We got in the car, and I immediately cranked it, making sure the A/C was on.

"Hungry?"

"Starving," he answered.

"Mom's making spaghetti tonight."

A faint nod.

Something wasn't right. Most of the time, any mention of Dixie's spaghetti was enough to snap my son out of even the worst mood. Instead, his face registered a sullen look as he kept his gaze through the passenger-side window of my car while we drove home.

"You practiced hard," I said, trying to gently prod around the edges. "Not many drops or bad passes, that I saw."

He said nothing.

"How was school today?"

"All right."

My mind kept fumbling through various possible problems.

"How's Milo?"

At this, I saw Jamie's chest heave as he took in a deep breath, and let out a deep sigh. "Good, I guess."

"What does that mean?" I probed. "Did you guys have a fight or something?"

"It's not that," he almost whispered.

"But it has something to do with Milo?" I followed up.

Jamie seemed to hesitate before answering.

"Son," I began, "if you don't want to talk about it, then we won't. But if it's something we can work on together, I'm willing to do it."

For the first time, Jamie turned and looked at me. "I almost got in a fight today."

I glanced at my son before turning back to face the road. "A fight?"

Jamie nodded. "With some kids who were picking on Milo."

"Oh," I said, as the pieces started to come together. "What were they doing to him?"

"Just talking sh...I mean, saying stuff."

I could not suppress a faint grin as I watched my son try to refrain from cursing in front of me.

"Calling him a 'retard,'" Jamie went on. "Asking if he was old enough to drive the short bus yet."

I felt my blood start to boil, as I pictured Milo sitting at Tootsie's with us, eating pizza and laughing as if he were a part of our family...which he was.

"That's awful," I said.

"That's not even the worst of it."

I looked at Jamie, as we stopped at a stoplight.

"Milo," he began, "said something about it afterward."

"What did he say?"

Jamie shook his head as if he did not want to talk about it anymore.

"He said that…that maybe he deserved it, because his parents didn't want him, and so maybe the guys were right for calling him that."

I felt sick to my stomach.

"Milo's had it rough his whole life," Jamie continued, "but no kid should have it that rough."

"No."

We drove on in silence…stunned silence; the cruelty of the world palpable like the thick, humid air outside my car.

"And so, what did you do?"

The soft features of Jamie's face hardened as he answered. "I told the main guy that I would beat the fuck…I mean, the crap out of him if he said anything else to Milo."

I now felt my blood go from boiling to filling my chest with pride, as I pictured my only son standing up for his friend.

"And then what happened?"

"He acted like he wanted to swing at me, but then he backed down…because he's a pussy."

I gave a faint grin. "Sounds like it."

"Still want Mom's spaghetti tonight, or would you rather go get a hamburger?"

Jamie gave me a quizzical look.

"You've earned it, I'd say," I told him, with a broad grin on my face.

Jamie smiled. "Let's just go home. I'm tired."

"You got it," I patted his arm.

We drove on in silence.

"Hey, Dad?" Jamie asked, after another moment.

"Yeah?"

"Can I ask you something?"

"Of course."

Jamie then hesitated. "Are there rules in college against non-players playing in games?"

I thought for a moment. "I believe so."

Jamie just nodded.

Following up, I said, "I haven't studied the rule book in depth, but I'm pretty sure the league forbids it."

"Yeah."

"Why do you ask?"

"Well," he began, "I think I might have an idea."

"Are you going to do it?" Dixie asked me, glancing up as we lay in bed together later that night.

"I don't know."

Dixie's deep green eyes bore into me, making me feel as if I had no choice but to say "yes."

"I want to," I answered her. "But I have to talk to Swicegood, first."

"So do I," Dixie responded. "I want to see it happen. I want to see Milo run that ball across the field during that opening game. I just hope it doesn't get squashed by Quinn or Charlie Stinson."

I shook my head. "I can't see either of them doing that, especially if it can drum up positive publicity for the program, which it can."

Both of us were silent for a moment.

"Jamie reminds me of you," I told her after a minute. "Not a hateful bone in his body."

"Mmmm," Dixie cooed in a playful tone, running a finger across my bare chest. "Are you saying that you have hateful bones in your body, then?"

"No," I answered. "But I am saying that I'm far less prone to compassion than you are."

Dixie frowned and gave my chest a gentle jab. "You've just let the football field harden you too much, Coach Leonard."

"Maybe that's it," I replied. "Blame the gridiron. How else can you explain how I treated you early on?"

"What do you mean 'early on'?" she asked, raising her head and looking at me.

"C'mon, don't pretend like you've forgotten middle and high school," I answered. "About how I walked down those halls day after day, ignoring you, my best friend from elementary school, who I used to climb jungle gyms with. And the only reason I did it was because of how far I could throw a leather ball."

Dixie frowned and laid her head back on my chest. "You're too hard on yourself, babe. Youth and teenage years are just that. They don't define a person."

"Which is what makes Jamie all the more remarkable," I rejoined. "Think about it: how many kids would stand up to a rabble of punk kids that were tormenting a boy with Down Syndrome, let alone *become best friends* with that boy?"

"You make a good point," Dixie agreed.

After another quiet moment, she spoke up again. "I got a call from Mom today."

"Yours or mine?"

"Mine."

"And?"

"She and Mike are coming up for the first game next week."

"That's awesome."

"It gets better."

I glanced down at her.

"Your mom is also coming up, along with the Gills."

"No way."

Dixie nodded her head.

"Brenda, Mike, Cheryl, Jim, and Jacqui Gill…are all coming up here for our first game?"

"And Jamie's," Dixie corrected me.

"Wow."

"All in Jim's new RV, too."

"What?!" I exclaimed, sitting up in bed, causing our bedsheet to shift.

Dixie covered her bare breasts and giggled at me. "You didn't know that Jim Gill bought a new RV after he retired?"

"No."

"It was a retirement present; from himself to himself, is how Mom described it."

"That's crazy."

"He and Jacqui have become quite the travelers in retirement, especially with Jordan off and busy with his own life. Going all over the place and finding deals on good hotels is one of their new hobbies."

I grinned and tried to picture Jim Gill—my lifelong friend from Lake Barrow, Florida, who had previously owned his car dealership—behind the wheel of an RV.

"From what Mom said, Jim found them a sweet price on a hotel just outside of Bowling Green for the trip up."

"Good for him."

"Are you excited?"

I laughed. "Between what we're hopefully doing for Milo and the Clampetts coming up from Lake Barrow, what's not to be excited about?"

Dixie gave me a playful tickle and kissed me as we turned out the lights.

Chapter 6

Season Opener: Yearwood State vs. Marquis State (Yearwood, KY)

Jakobe Ackerman and Connor Judd had joined Swicegood and me in a small equipment room off to the side of the main locker room.

"We wanted to let you guys know first, before we said anything to the team," Swicegood began.

Both of them had been getting suited up when we had called them in. Jakobe wore his football pants and a Spandex undershirt, while Connor had already donned his shoulder pads and jersey, with the number 16.

Both knew why we had called them in.

"We're going with Jakobe," Swicegood stated.

Jakobe gave a slight nod, almost as if he knew he would get the nod for today. Truth was, most people did know.

As for Connor, he too acknowledged the decision with a head nod and seemed to have expected this.

"This wasn't easy," I added, keeping my eyes on Connor. "Doesn't matter what the papers say, or anyone else…rumors, whatever. Both of you guys had great spring and summer workouts, and Connor, you've got nothing to be ashamed of."

"Yes sir," he answered.

"Truth is, we're in a great spot," Swicegood continued. "Having both of you ready to take snaps gives us an edge, especially if—God forbid—something should happen to Jakobe."

I watched Connor, whose expression was now difficult to read.

Swicegood dismissed the two men, who turned to go back to the locker room.

"Connor, you good?" I asked.

"Yes sir," he stated in a sincere voice. "I'm good."

I nodded, convinced. "Keep pushing," I encouraged him. "You'll get your shot someday."

Connor stood facing me, his muscular frame taking up most of the doorway, as he gave me a faint—almost sly–grin.

"I know I will," he told me.

His response left me puzzled.

"YOU SURE ABOUT THIS?!" Swicegood yelled at me over the din of thousands of fans stomping and screaming above us. "This thing with the Milo kid?"

We were in the tunnel just under the stadium and were about to run onto the field for our first game of the season. I could barely hear him over the noise, which was generated by 30,000 fans, many of whom had been ready for football season since December of the previous year.

"You signed off on it," I answered.

"Kind of wondering if I should have or not."

"Long as Charlie Stinson's okay with it, then I guess we should be too," I added with a grin. "He's the boss."

"Shut the hell up," Swicegood snapped.

I laughed.

Milo, it's your big day, I thought to myself, leaning into the excitement that was all around us.

As we stood in the tunnel, the energy was palpable as the team prepared to run onto Mustang Field for the 2019 season.

Still, a large part of my mind was on the previous evening.

Jamie's first outing as a starting high school quarterback the night before had been tremendous. He had thrown for three touchdowns and over two hundred and fifty yards. And he had done it all in front of a large group of family and friends that had traveled up from Lake Barrow, Florida to watch him. After my game, we would be meeting them for an early dinner at Tootsie's.

"How's Connor?" Swicegood asked me, interrupting the memory.

"He's fine," I said with a nod.

"Not every day you get told you're going to be the second-string quarterback."

"He took it fine," I answered. "It's his uncle that's going to be pissed."

Swicegood chuckled and shook his head. "Let him be pissed."

"Let's go Mustangs!"

"Hoo!"

"Let's go!"

"Hoo!"

"Let's go!"

"Hoo!"

Adalius Bennett, our top linebacker, led the hype as the team got ready to sprint out of the tunnel and onto the field. All seventy-four of our players began bouncing around inside the tunnel. The metallic sound of their cleats hitting the concrete floor was barely audible over the bedlam that was unfolding just above them.

The energy was intense, and will always be one of my favorite parts of the game, and my involvement with it.

As Adalius tore through the tunnel entrance, the rest of the team trailed him, and our coaching staff was not far behind. The noise seemed to intensify—if that was even possible—as we bolted through the end zone and sprinted toward our sideline.

The 2019 season was underway.

I got to the sideline and began looking into the stands for Jamie and Milo.

Normally, I would be up in the coaches' booth, high above the field, where I would call down plays to Swicegood, who would relay them to our players on the field.

Today was not a normal day, though.

"Dad!" I heard Jamie call out.

I turned and waved at my son. Milo was next to him and had a smile that seemed to be as wide as the field itself. I only hoped he had not caught on to what we were doing.

Katie, our team manager, along with a uniformed security officer, opened the gate to our sideline on the field, and let the boys in. Both of them strode up to where I was standing on the sideline.

"Coach Jayce!" Milo exclaimed, his excitement seeming to ooze through his face. "Jamie said we're going to be with the players here!"

"That's right," I affirmed. "You excited?"

He didn't need to answer, but squealed, "Yeah!"

We had won the coin toss and elected to receive. As the kicking team for Marquis State got set, our receiving team took their positions on the field.

The excitement continued to rise, as the other team's kicker bolted forward, and booted the ball high in the air toward the opposite end zone, where Deon Flowers, our kick returner, waited to field it.

As the ball hung in the air, I could almost feel the collective breath of the crowd being held. Deon caught it as it came down. Up the field he ran, reaching just beyond the thirty-yard line before he was tackled.

I turned to Katie, who was standing nearby, and whispered, "You got the helmet?"

She nodded and grinned. The entire team was in on "the Milo project," as I had heard a few players refer to it.

Ladies and gentlemen, may I have your attention, please? came the voice of our announcer over the loudspeaker.

The crowd noise died down, but only somewhat.

The announcer continued: *Although today's game has just begun, we would like to pause for a moment and recognize a very special honorary player for the Yearwood State Mustangs in today's contest with Marquis State. This young man has continually demonstrated his dedication and loyalty to the Mustangs for years, and today, we would like to reward that with a very special moment for him.*

At this time, ladies and gentlemen, please join me in congratulating...MILO CRENSHAW...and welcoming him as he joins the mighty Mustangs of Yearwood State on the field!

The crowd began cheering loudly again, and several of the players walked over to where Milo was standing with Jamie.

Milo's face was a picture of bewilderment, ecstasy, and disbelief.

"What?!" he asked.

"You ready to run the ball, Milo?" I asked him, trying to contain my excitement.

"Run the ball?!" he exclaimed.

"Yeah, man," Adalius Bennet beamed, giving Milo a gentle punch in the arm. "It's your day to be a superstar! You ready to go out there and score against Marquis State?"

Milo's jaw dropped, and he was speechless.

"Let's go, Milo!" bellowed Russell Villemont, our defensive lineman as he jumped up on one of the sideline benches and facing the crowd.

"Milo! Milo! Milo!" he began chanting.

The rest of our sideline—players, coaches, and Katie—picked up on it, and began chanting as well.

"Milo! Milo! Milo!"

Before long, several of the fans had joined in, and within moments, the sound of Milo's name being chanted rang high above the capacity crowd at Mustang Field.

Katie had been holding a small helmet, just big enough for Milo to wear. She walked over to him and cinched it over his head, helping him buckle the chin strap.

Milo looked out at the field with deep excitement and bravado, where our first-team offense was beckoning for him to join them.

Swicegood and I had fixed it with Marquis State's team and coaches, as well as the officiating crew, and even some of the league brass. All of us had determined that, despite the rules saying that no non-player should come onto the field of play during an actual contest, an exception could be made here, since it was only for one "play," if that was even the word.

And so, as Milo sprinted onto the field for that first play against Marquis State, we all stood and looked on with happiness while the crowd roared. I turned and glanced into the stands. Folks had their phones out; most were recording, all were cheering, and a few had tears in their eyes. I looked for Dixie and our crew from Florida, but could not find them.

The offense got set. The linemen and receivers took their positions, and Jakobe, along with Downtown Mathias Brown flanking him on one side in the shotgun and Milo on the other, began to call out cadence. He bellowed "hut," and Clay Moss snapped the ball to him.

Marquis State's defensive players and our offensive linemen made pantomimed gestures at hitting each other, as Jakobe handed the ball off to Milo, who took the ball and froze up. There he stood next to our quarterback, unsure of what to do next.

Then I heard Jakobe call out, "Run!"

At this, Milo took off.

His foot speed was minimal, and I figured that was a combination of his lack of natural quickness, as well as the shock that he still felt at being on our field. Still, his desire was there as he bolted up the middle, right between Marquis State's defenders and our offensive linemen, who were pretending to grapple. A few defenders—in on what we were doing—reached out as if to grab Milo and tackle him.

But Milo ran through them, which seemed to embolden him. As each of Marquis State's linebackers, and a few defensive backs, ran to him and pretended to try tackling him, Milo dodged each of them.

Soon, he was in the open field, and the crowd roared even louder; their chants of "Milo! Milo! Milo!" creating a cauldron of noise as he sprinted toward the end zone about fifty yards away.

"Milo! Milo! Milo! Milo! Milo!"

Swicegood and I ambled down our sideline with grins on our faces, along with several of our players, as we kept our eyes on Milo while he ran to glory.

Now, our offensive linemen, followed by Jakobe, Deon Flowers, Downtown, and others were coming up behind him. They sprinted ahead and formed a convoy around Milo as he neared the end zone, his helmet gleaming in the early afternoon sun.

Milo reached the twenty-yard line, then the fifteen, then the ten, and the crowd noise rose in its intensity with each step he took toward his moment in the spotlight.

Finally, Milo Crenshaw—a fifteen-year-old boy with Down Syndrome, health problems, and a life of misfortune—crossed the goal line, and was immediately mobbed by our offensive team. For a moment, it was impossible to see him, as he was enshrouded within a cluster of blue and gold jerseys.

A moment later, however, we saw him; Cam Grigsby and Clay Moss, or two best linemen, had hoisted him up onto their shoulders, and Milo immediately unsnapped his helmet and raised it in the air as he yelled triumphantly at the sky.

It was an image I knew I would never forget as long as I lived.

Sports can be a painful racket; it can be deceptive; it can be dishonest; and it can be exhilarating. But I learned—or perhaps was reminded—on that day about how sports can call out our best selves, even amid humanity's worst tendencies and moments.

Mustang Field, for one moment on one day, was no longer a football stadium, it was a sanctuary; a safe haven for the human spirit.

Soul Rasheed, my late close friend, would have been proud.

Milo was carried over to the sideline and was let down right in front of me.

"You did it, Milo," I beamed at him. "You ran for a touchdown."

"I know," he responded, breathing heavily and grinning from ear to ear.

"How was it?"

Milo did not answer right away and seemed to think long and hard before answering.

"Best day of my life!" he exclaimed.

CHAPTER 7

We beat Marquis State by a score of 42-14.

Jakobe was spectacular at quarterback, throwing for two touchdowns and running for another. Downtown Mathias Brown added a score of his own, and our defense and punt return teams contributed two touchdowns as well. Chris Whiteside picked off Marquis State's quarterback and ran it back for a score, while Deon Flowers ran a punt return sixty-three yards for the final touchdown of the afternoon.

All this on top of Milo's moment in the spotlight made it a game to remember.

In the locker room, the team celebrated with raucous music and lots of whooping and hollering. I stood back, along with Swicegood, and just took it all in.

"You coming to the presser with me?" Swicegood leaned over and yelled into my ear.

"Sure," I said.

"I'd personally rather stay here," Swicegood added as if he could read my mind.

"Let's go," I told him in a begrudging tone.

We left the locker room and immediately saw Katie standing there. She lit up when she saw us—or so we thought—but it did not take long for me to realize that she was smiling at the person *behind us.*

I turned and saw Jakobe Ackerman as he walked behind us. He went over and, without seeing us, embraced Katie, who was equally oblivious to our presence.

"You stunk it up out there," she insulted him in a playful tone.

Jakobe scoffed as he put his arm around her. "Might have done better if I had a better tutor," he replied. "Got me so worried about my grades, I can't even concentrate out there."

"That's a lame excuse," she flirted.

Swicegood and I exchanged glances. "Hope that doesn't get complicated," he said as we walked. "Romance and football don't mix."

"I know some coaches' wives who would disagree with that," I replied.

"I know some divorced coaches who wouldn't."

Five minutes later, Swicegood was standing behind a podium in front of a backdrop that was decorated with our team's logo. I stood off to the side beyond the press pool.

"Coach Leonard," came a deep, southern voice.

I turned and tried not to frown when I saw who was behind me.

"Mr. Stinson," I said, managing a warm smile.

Charlie Stinson was taller than me by several inches and had a way of filling up your personal space when he addressed you, whether he meant to or not. That day, he wore a white, button-down shirt with the Yearwood State logo stitched on the right breast, tan khakis, a pair of loafers, and a large brown sun hat. A broad smile spread across his weather-beaten face as he spoke to me.

"Helluva game today," he affirmed.

"We got it done."

"Sure was a good thing you all did for that little fella, too," he said, referring to Milo.

I nodded. "It was my son's idea."

"So I heard."

At the podium, Swicegood was talking about the play of Jakobe Ackerman. Charlie frowned.

"I hear that boy of yours, Jamie," Charlie continued, "is as humble as they come. He sure reminds me of Connor when he was that age."

I didn't look at him.

"Talented, too," Charlie added.

I nodded.

"Damn shame Connor's not on that field this year, Jayce," Charlie added.

"He'll get his moment," I offered.

"He deserves it," Charlie shot back, fixing my eyes with his. "You know as well as I do that Ackerman kid got the job based on his coming from an elite program."

"That's not true."

Charlie scoffed and looked in the direction of Swicegood before averting his eyes.

"You're a good coach, Jayce," Charlie said. "Even better, you're level-headed; and able to be reasoned with. The same can't be said for Jeff Swicegood, and you know it. Fact is, he's too damn head-strong to realize when he's made a mistake."

"You think he's made a mistake by going with Jakobe at quarterback?"

"He never gave Connor a fair shot," Charlie rejoined. "Everyone knows it."

I shook my head and was about to protest when Charlie cut me off.

"You're the offensive coordinator; therefore, you've got some pull in that locker room."

I gave Charlie a quizzical look.

"Connor deserves a shot," Charlie began, "and your son's team deserves some new digs."

"What are you saying?" I pressed him.

"I'm saying that I can make it worth your while if you can make things work for Connor. He deserves it, Jayce and no one knows it better than you."

I turned so that my body was squared with his. "You're bribing me?"

Charlie's hardened expression softened a bit, and a thin smile creased his lips.

"I'm a guy you want in your corner, Coach Leonard, for better or worse. Sometimes being on the right team can be a tricky thing. But you owe it to yourself to figure out which team that is."

With that, he turned and began walking out with the same slow, meandering gait that befitted rich guys his age.

He went a few steps, then turned and faced me again.

"You think about what I've said, Coach."

Tootsie's was hopping after the game that afternoon. Even after all these years, and being under new management, it was still the destination of choice for Yearwood State football fans before, during, and after home games.

I made my way inside, scanned the dining area, and soon found our group's table.

"There he is!" Jim Gill called out from a long table in the corner, waving me over.

I smiled and headed that way, trying all the while to push the image of Charlie Stinson and our conversation from my psyche.

66

"Give that man a round of applause for a game well called!" Jim led the charge, as everyone at the table began clapping for me.

"Stop!" I dismissed before I greeted everyone.

"Hey, darling!" my mother, Cheryl Leonard, stood up slowly to kiss me on the cheek. It had been over twenty years since a drunk driver had hit her while she checked the mailbox at her workplace, leaving her hip shattered, and her ability to walk decimated. But she was in good health. Her once-brown hair was almost fully gray, and she was showing other signs of aging but was still in good spirits and good health. Her radiant, glowing smile was still the same.

I hugged Jim Gill next. He was an old man now; far from the middle-aged patriarch of one of Lake Barrow's wealthiest families, as I always remembered him. He got around well but definitely looked like the grandpa he now was (thanks to Jordan, his youngest son, now a married father). Jacqui Gill, his wife, was aging too, and was doing so gracefully; her jet-black hair showed signs of gray, but mostly remained its natural color.

Seeing the two of them, I often wondered what their oldest son, Jamie, my best friend who had been killed in Afghanistan back in 2002, would look like today if he were still alive.

"Proud of you and your team," Jim congratulated me.

"Thanks," I said.

I then greeted Dixie's mother and stepfather; Mike and Brenda Stovall. Both of them hugged me and congratulated me as well.

Dixie then kissed me and told me she was proud of me. Jamie and Milo were enraptured by a video game on Jamie's phone, though my son did give me a nod as I sat down.

I was seated between Jim and Dixie and began looking at a menu. Soon, Max came and began taking orders.

"Waiter duty?" I asked him.

"We're short-staffed today," Max replied with a shrug.

"So is Jayce," Jim cut in, giving Max a wry grin. "He could use some help on the sideline, kinda like you gave him back in Sims County years ago."

Max gave Jim a faint smile and nodded. It was a cool response that was not lost on me.

When Max had left, Jim turned to me. "He still doesn't like me much."

I shrugged. "Max is Max."

"Guess I can't blame him," Jim said, his wrinkled brow furrowing. "After the way I treated you way back then, Jayce…"

"Don't, Jim," I assured him. "It's in the past."

Jim gave a rueful nod.

The friendship between myself and Jim Gill, though strong, had not always been without trial and disagreement. Jim had stepped in and become like a second father to me after my own stepfather had passed away years earlier. He had done so again when Mom had her accident with the drunk driver. When her medical bills had almost prevented me from accepting a scholarship to play football at Yearwood State, Jim had emerged with a job offer for Mom to make good money with benefits, thus freeing me up from the burden of having to stay home and work to support her. For that, I have been—and will always be—grateful.

Then Soul Rasheed became part of our lives, and Jim's friendship with me almost ended. Soul came to Lake Barrow to coach with me in 2003, much to the chagrin of Jim Gill and several others. 9/11 had happened less than two years earlier, Jamie had been killed in Afghanistan, and Jim had viewed Soul's Muslim faith as a deal-breaker, regardless of how good a football coach he had proved to be.

Through a series of deliberate manipulations and false accusations, Jim had nearly succeeded in getting Soul (and me) fired from our jobs before our first year of coaching had finished. As a wealthy business owner and pillar of the community, he'd had that power, and I hate to think of how things might have turned out if his plan had succeeded.

Of course, what kept it from succeeding was far more devastating and heart-breaking than perhaps any job loss I might have endured. When Soul had been killed by a gunman at our school that same year, it soon came to light that he had lost his life by protecting Jordan Gill, Jim's only remaining son, from the shooter.

From then on, Soul had been—rightly—hailed as a hero, and Jim had repented of his ways. Our friendship had survived all of it, and I was thankful.

"How's retired life?" I asked him.

"Never better," he said, taking a sip from his water glass. "Jacqui and I have spent more time in that RV than we have at home this year."

I chuckled. "You've earned it."

"Dealership's in good hands," he added, "so I'd probably have to agree with you."

"Who's running it now?"

"You didn't hear?"

I shook my head.

Jim smirked. "Who's the last person you'd expect to be running Jim Gill Automotive."

I thought for a moment. "Marty Danforth."

"You're very close."

I gave Jim an incredulous stare. "Matt Danforth?"

"Bingo."

"You're kidding me."

"Nope."

"How in the world did you make that happen?"

"Matt's a qualified guy," Jim shrugged. "He'd been working for his daddy's company since he came back to Lake Barrow about ten years ago, and he just took over the dealership for me in the last year."

I laughed again and shook my head. A Danforth working anywhere near a Gill was unheard of in Sims County about twenty years earlier. This was due to a long-standing feud and controversy between the two wealthy families that dated back to 1990 and involved a disputed piece of land.

And yet, in 2019, Matt Danforth, Marty's son, was now operating Jim Gill Automotive, and I marveled once more at how things can always change for the better.

"You okay?" Jim asked me moments later. "You seem kinda distant."

"Just tired from the game," I answered, hoping Jim would leave it at that.

He kept his eyes on me. "You used to crash at our house on Friday nights after big games, back when you and Jamie played," Jim said, keeping his eye on me. "I got to know you pretty well during those years, Jayce, which is why I know the difference between you being tired, and you having something on your mind besides football."

I managed a grin. "Just some stuff with some boosters."

"I know a thing or two about that," Jim gave an embarrassed chuckle. "You do too, unfortunately. Coming from Lake Barrow, you've dealt with the biggest pain in the ass to ever host a fundraiser."

"Don't be too hard on yourself, Jim," I replied. "You've got nothing on this guy."

"Who is he?"

"Rich dude whose nephew isn't starting at quarterback."

Jim grimaced.

I then told him about what Charlie Stinson had said to me. Jim listened, and when I was finished, he was quiet for a moment.

"You've always had a backbone, Jayce," he finally broke the silence. "Even when I tried to break it, you never let me. Soul Rasheed's coming to Lake Barrow was the perfect example. You knew he would be a helluva coach, and sure enough, he was."

I nodded in agreement.

"Football's an amazing sport," Jim continued. "I've always loved it, especially when you and Jamie were making memories together in high school. But it can get ugly too, as you well know."

"I know."

Jim then locked eyes with me. "That's why you need to stand your ground," he said. "This rich guy you've got in your ear may take your job one day, but don't ever let him take your integrity."

"I won't."

"Because the only way you can lose that is if you give it away."

CHAPTER 8

The next Friday, Jamie had an away game about a half hour outside of town. Thankfully, I was able to see this one, thanks to our Saturday game being at home that weekend.

Dixie and I arrived at the stadium, purchased tickets, and made our way inside the gate. As is usually the case with away games, the visitors' bleachers were smaller than the hometown team's, and yet I was surprised to see the number of Yearwood fans that had trekked to the small burg of Westwood, Kentucky. We were heavily favored that night, even with Jamie starting at quarterback as a freshman.

Milo was with us and, after buying him a hot dog and a Sprite, we found our seats. Earlier we had picked him up from his grandmother's house and had spent the trip listening to him chatter about anything and everything that was on his mind. It had been almost a week since he had run the ball for Yearwood State, and the glow of that moment was still very much upon him.

"How's the dog, Milo?" I asked, sitting next to him.

His mouth was full, and he replied to me with a thumbs-up.

I grinned and continued watching the field, where Jamie was warming up.

Soon, I felt a tap on my shoulder. I turned.

"Nothing like a Friday night getaway into the boondocks, huh?" Quinn Howser grinned as he took a seat next to me.

"Quieter than Yearwood," I answered, shaking my athletic director's hand. "Especially the night before a home game."

"Gonna be ready for Ohio Christian tomorrow?" he asked.

I nodded. "I think so."

A grin spread across Howser's wide face.

"Kenzie cheering tonight?" I asked.

"Of course," he answered, pointing to the field down below where Yearwood High's cheer squad was warming up. Howser's daughter was a junior captain on the squad. "How's Jamie adjusting to high school so far?" he asked.

"So far so good," I told him. "Almost been in a fight already."

Howser gave me a surprised look, and I told him about the incident with Milo and the bullies.

"Wow," he said when I had finished. "Jamie's got real balls."

I chuckled at the expression and nodded my agreement.

"Gives you hope for this generation, doesn't it?" Howser added.

"I'd say so."

"Plenty of posers and bullies out there, that's for sure."

We were silent for a moment.

"Hey, about the game tomorrow," Howser finally said, "Do you think we'll get to see Connor Judd take the field?"

I bristled and replied with, "I don't know."

"I don't have to tell you why I'm asking, do I?"

"Like you said, lots of bullies out there," I quipped.

"It's not just your ass Stinson stays on, Jayce," Howser continued, reading my frustration. "Or Swicegood's for that matter. He holds a lot of sway over the purse strings, and as it turns out, his nephew plays quarterback for our team."

As much as I liked Connor Judd, I found myself wishing at that moment, that Swicegood would have left him the hell alone, instead of recruiting him out of high school.

"Do you trust our decision?" I pressed Howser.

"Of course I do."

I held up my hands as if to say, *"Well then..."*

"You and Swicegood know quarterbacks better than any duo I've ever hired," Howser continued. "But it's my job to operate the business side of things."

I nodded and glanced over at Milo, who sat next to Dixie and appeared to be finishing off his Sprite. Both of them were fixated on the field and were oblivious to what we were discussing.

"Just promise me this," Howser told me. "Promise me that you'll try to work Judd in some more. He doesn't have to play a lot, but bring him in for special situations here and there. It's the only way to keep Charlie Stinson on a leash."

"And Charlie Stinson's money flowing into the coffers."

"Exactly."

I shook my head and stared off into the distance. If there was one thing I hated, it was micro-management. And the bitch of it, right at that moment, was that Quinn Howser, my boss, wasn't even the one micro-managing. Instead, a rich guy who wasn't even physically present and who had no official position within our football program was pulling the puppet strings.

I felt my heart begin to race, and my cheeks begin to get hot.

Jim Gill was my friend, and we were on good terms after all that had transpired between us years earlier. But as I sat listening to Quinn Howser tell me how to do my job, my mind went back to those days when it was Jim micro-managing things back in Lake Barrow. It was a painful flashback, and one I knew I would probably never be fully rid of.

"I gotta get back to Kathy," Howser said, getting up. "Just think about what I said."

I did not respond.

"For what it's worth, Jayce," Howser added, turning to me, "you probably ought to consider what I've said especially because of what we know about Jakobe Ackerman."

I turned and glared at him. "Meaning what?"

"You know what I mean?" Howser responded. "The reason he transferred to us from Louisville."

"I know about the sexual assault accusations," I retorted. "You think you're telling me something I don't know?"

"Just be careful."

I turned back to the field.

"Be careful who you trust, Jayce."

The game started and Yearwood jumped out to a 21-0 lead over Westwood before halftime. Jamie played decently, but did have an interception and a fumble, which the other team recovered. On the sideline, however, his poise seemed to be steady, which I was glad to see.

As halftime got underway, and the bands began their show, I got up to head to the restroom and stretch my legs a bit.

My phone vibrated in my pocket.

I fished it out and glanced at Jeff Swicegood's name on the screen before answering it.

"Yeah?"

"Jayce, sorry to bother you. I know you're at Jamie's game."

"No problem. Halftime just started."

"Good, because I need to talk to you."

"What's up?"

"We've got a problem." Jeff Swicegood's voice was steady, but I could sense that he was uneasy.

"What problem?" I asked, bracing for the worst.

Swicegood took a deep breath. "It's Jakobe," he finally said. "He's been accused of sexual assault."

I stopped dead in my tracks in front of the restroom entrance.

"By Katie Corvin, our team manager."

CHAPTER 9

"It's all lies, man," Jakobe Ackerman said, as we sat in Swicegood's office the next morning. "I barely even saw Katie at that party. I can't believe she's lyin' on me like this!"

At that moment, our team was only hours from taking on Ohio Christian College.

"Just tell us your side," Swicegood pressed. "All the facts."

Jakobe shifted his tall, muscular frame in the chair he sat in, a look of indignation on his face. He ran his fingers through his dreadlocks, and took a deep breath as he straightened his tie; game-day attire, along with the button-down shirt and khakis he wore.

"It was last week," he began. "The night after the Marquis State game. A whole bunch of the frat houses had this big party, and everyone was invited. I mean, *everyone*. Didn't matter who you were; if you were on campus, you could go."

Jakobe paused and appeared to be thinking of how to continue.

"So..." Swicegood prodded.

"So we went."

"Who's 'we'?"

"A bunch of the guys," Jakobe added. "Me, Flowers, Downtown Brown, Del McLelland; a whole bunch of us."

"And Katie," I clarified.

"I mean, yeah, she was there."

"But nothing happened?" I asked.

"No," he asserted in a defensive tone. "Not with me."

"Did you see anybody else with her?" Swicegood asked.

"I can't remember."

"Were you drunk?"

"I had some drinks, yeah," Jakobe answered.

"Not enough to pass out, or anything?"

"No, I didn't pass out."

Swicegood and I exchanged glances.

"So what happens now?" Jakobe asked. "Do I still get to play?"

Swicegood hesitated before answering, the uncertainty in his face visible.

"You're playing," he said after a moment. "We'll see how things shake out, but for now, you're in."

"I can go get suited up, then?" Jakobe stood.

"Yeah."

Jakobe left, and the two of us remained in the office. Swicegood leaned back in his chair, took a deep breath, and rubbed his eyes.

I kept my eyes on him. "Do you believe his story?"

"I have no reason to not believe him," Swicegood said. "Just like I've got no reason to not believe Katie. That's why we're letting the investigation unfold before benching Jakobe, or whatever else we need to do."

I nodded, feeling every bit of the tension and uncertainty that Swicegood seemed to be shouldering at that moment.

"Have you talked to Katie?" I asked.

Swicegood seemed to wince. "I talked to her on the phone earlier today," he answered. "We agreed that it might be best if she wasn't involved with the team, at least for a while."

"How is she?"

"Rough."

"Is she getting care of any kind?"

"She's been talking to a victim's advocate with the university. Darcy's office," Swicegood said. "That's all I know."

I sighed. The euphoria of the previous week all of a sudden seemed years away.

Ohio Christian University proved to be a more formidable opponent than anticipated.

Jakobe was definitely off. Late in the fourth quarter, with the score sitting at 24-21 in our favor, we were hoping to get at least another score to pad our lead.

Instead, Jakobe threw an interception, and the Ohio Christian defender ran it back to within our thirty-yard line, setting them up to get at least a game-tying field goal. From there, Ohio Christian's offense drove to within the ten-yard line and was poised to put it in the end zone.

Miraculously, their quarterback fumbled the next snap from under center, and we recovered with forty-five seconds left.

Once our offense had taken the field again, Jakobe took a knee and ran the clock out, giving us one of the ugliest wins that I had ever been a part of, certainly as a coach at Yearwood State.

In the locker room following the game, the atmosphere was nowhere near as upbeat as it had been during the Marquis State game. Our guys were relieved, yet subdued. And I could not blame them. We had nearly lost at home to an opponent that most media outlets had us beating by at least three touchdowns.

Things did not get any better for us during the post-game press conference.

"Coach Swicegood," asked one cub reporter from a Lexington outlet, "what is your assessment of the performance of your team against Ohio Christian?"

Standing at the dais, Swicegood looked exhausted. He took a moment to consider the question before answering.

His response was measured; *it wasn't our best performance, with plenty of mistakes, but I'm proud of the team for coming together and getting the win, even if it was an ugly win.*

He paused as the journalists took notes.

"Coach, one question about the quarterback situation," said another reporter. "Obviously, with Jakobe Ackerman struggling today, did you ever feel the need to replace him with Connor Judd?"

Swicegood shot back without hesitation. "Jakobe Ackerman is our quarterback."

Another stood up and asked, "Coach, there have been rumors that recent locker room issues may be contributing to some division within the team, as well as affecting the play of the team on the field. Specifically, I'm referring to the division over the choice you have to make between the two quarterbacks. Can you comment on any of this?"

Swicegood almost cut him off before he could finish. "I have no comment on that. I'm not going to dignify that garbage. Next question."

We had a good practice on Monday; better than expected. The guys were focused, and seemed to have gotten a wake-up call from the near-miss we'd had against Ohio Christian.

Jakobe's passes seemed more on-point, which caused us both to breathe easier.

After practice, we huddled up and Swicegood addressed the team. I watched him with quiet admiration. Jeff Swicegood could be a hard-ass when he needed to be, but he also knew his team, as well as the generation we now coached. I had seen the careers of too many older coaching colleagues end prematurely for never understanding the importance of answering the "why" questions. "Do-it-because-I-said-do-it" seldom worked with the younger generation anymore, and coaches who did not adapt their style to this reality often ended up on the outs.

"Any questions?" Swicegood asked the team, once he had finished his brief remarks.

"Yeah," Clint Gaines asked. "Is Katie off the team?"

Some of our guys giggled, while others murmured. The noise made my blood boil, and put me on alert, to see if any inappropriate remarks would be made. As far as I was concerned, Katie was already an innocent victim in all of this, no matter what Jakobe, or anyone, had done or not done.

"Katie is taking a break right now," Swicegood gave a simple answer. "She is not with the team, and we'll just see what happens."

More stifled laughter, as several players exchanged knowing glances. The rumors had already been circulating.

"Slut, slut," I heard a freshman player say to a teammate next to him. He had tried to mouth the words under his breath, but I heard him and was also able to read his lips.

I strode over to where he was kneeling at the back of the crowd, stood behind him, and bent down.

"If I ever," I growled into his ear, "hear you denigrate Katie or any other woman or girl like that again, I'm going to kick your ass across this field so hard, you'll think you're headed straight through the uprights to score us three points."

For a moment, he acted as though he wanted to push back and respond. Then he saw my face, backed down, and said nothing.

"And you better pass the word, too," I added, loudly enough for the rest of the team to hear. "Because the same thing goes for anyone on this team that I hear being disrespectful of women. Understood."

"Yes sir."

I stood back up and glanced at Swicegood who had taken notice of the exchange. He grinned at me from behind his sunglasses.

Sometimes it pays to be a hard-ass, I thought to myself.

CHAPTER 10

*H*i, *this is Katie. Sorry, I missed your call. Gimme a shout when you hear the beep, and I'll call you right back. Thanks. Bye.*

It was later that day after practice, and I was in the car headed home…worried.

I had been fighting with myself over whether or not to even call Katie following the game on Saturday. She was every bit a member of our team, not to mention a member of my own family. And all I wanted was to hear her voice.

But what would I say to her? What if I made it worse? What if she blames me for what happened?

I heard the tone signaling for me to talk and felt my insides tense up.

Why had I dialed the damned number without knowing ahead of time what I was going to say?

I hesitated for a moment before hanging up. She would see my number, and know that I had called, but would not hear me bumbling like an idiot on the phone.

I drove on toward home…praying.

Dixie and I had barely spoken since Friday night when I had first gotten the call about the allegations. She was angry, and justifiably so. Not only was sexual assault involved, but it also involved Katie.

I entered the house and did not see her right away. We were at a point in our marriage where I no longer expected to see her waiting nearby when I walked through the door. And so, it did not surprise me to find her upstairs reading a book in bed. She was in casual wear – jeans and a t-shirt – and gave me a faint smile as I entered.

"Hey," she offered. Indifferent tone; the sort that conveyed that she was upset but not yet ready to let it fly unhindered.

"How's your day been?" I asked her.

"Fine," she said. Then, almost reading my mind, she added, "Jamie's over at Milo's. He'll be home soon."

"Really?" I checked my watch. Almost 7:30. "It's a school night."

"I know," she replied in a sharp tone as if warning me about pushing the issue of "responsibility" on her part. "What's the latest with Jakobe?" she pressed.

I was disarmed, yet had found myself in a defensive posture.

"Nothing new," I said. "Investigation is underway."

"Is he playing Saturday?"

"As of now, yes."

Dixie looked away, and I saw the consternation and disappointment in her face.

"What am I supposed to do, Dixie? It's Swicegood's decision."

I stood there as if facing a firing squad.

Dixie read my misery and watched me suffer for a few moments as I stood in the doorway to our bedroom. When she finally spoke, she said, "You have more influence there than you're willing to admit right now. And you've always done the right thing, Jayce. Please don't let this incident be the one exception where you don't."

I could not think of anything to say but managed a faint nod.

"Do right by Katie."

"Have you heard from her?" I asked.

"I've been calling. No answer."

Tennessee Central College was our next opponent. We trounced them 48-7. As it turned out, they were the perfect opponent for us that week, given all that had happened. Our level of competition was only going to get stiffer as the season wore on, and having a cupcake team to whale on beforehand helped our team's confidence.

Jakobe was the perfect example of this. He lit up TCC's defense to the tune of 20 for 25 passing, 382 yards, and 4 touchdowns. He had no interceptions.

It was a tremendous bounce-back game for our team, which is probably why no one saw what happened next.

At the press conference, Swicegood took a few softball questions about the game, all of which he answered with ease.

Then, a reporter who worked for an outlet that had no business covering our game stood up and spoke.

"Coach, can you comment on the rumors of sexual assault surrounding your quarterback, Jakobe Ackerman?"

Swicegood looked stunned. It was an ambush, and neither he nor I (nor anyone else) was ready for it.

CHAPTER 11

"It was bound to get out sooner or later," I told Swicegood, as we stood in his office overlooking the field a half hour after the press conference.

Swicegood glared at me. "Not like this," he growled.

"'No defensive scheme can stop the papers,'" I replied, quoting a favorite saying of his.

Jeff Swicegood was having none of it. "You can't tell me that little bitty paper, which never covers us, suddenly got interested in a story that they should have had no access to in the first place."

I could think of nothing to say in response. He had a point, and both of us knew it.

"Something's not right," he said, rising out of his chair and going to his window.

Outside, the grounds crew was still cleaning up the field and the custodians were picking up trash in the bleachers. Swicegood seemed to stare past them.

"Do you think someone is trying to hurt the program by leaking the Ackerman story?"

"Either that or they're trying to hurt us," he said.

"Who?" I asked.

Swicegood's back was to me. He shook his head. "I don't even want to think about those possibilities."

There was a knock at the door, and Swicegood called for whoever it was to enter.

The door opened and in walked Quinn Howser. Charlie Stinson was trailing behind him.

"Afternoon, gentlemen," he said.

"Why are you here?" Swicegood snarled, looking past Howser and glaring at Stinson.

Stinson made no verbal reply but gave a faint smirk at the angry reaction his presence produced.

"Jeff, calm down," Howser tried to soothe. "Listen, we were all taken aback by the surprise question…"

"By a paper that had no business even being there," I cut in.

"I know it," Howser snapped at me. "And it shouldn't have happened. But it did, and now we need to talk about damage control."

"Meaning what?" I asked.

Howser and Stinson were both looking at Swicegood, who was steaming.

Stinson led off. "Can I make a suggestion?"

"I'm in no mood," Swicegood snarled, "to listen to whatever bullshit order—disguised as a suggestion—you're planning to shove in my face."

"Just hear him out," Howser ordered.

Stinson cleared his throat and began, "I have a solution that may help now that the cat's out of the bag. The truth is that you're playing a guy who already has a sexual assault record coming out of Louisville. So, here's my solution. And it's really simple: you let Connor start the home games you have coming up, and Jakobe can start the away games."

"What?" Swicegood was incredulous.

"Here's why," Howser picked up. "A lot of important people around here, both in administration and in the boosters, are going to be pissed now that they know that Jakobe—already with a sexual assault case hanging over him in his past—now has this new one while he's wearing a uniform for our team. Sitting him for home games will allow things to blow over, and will also give Connor some playing time."

I considered this for a moment, in contrast to Swicegood, who seemed to recoil at what he was hearing.

"Jeff, it's a far better idea than sitting Jakobe entirely in favor of Connor," Howser urged. "And it beats the heck out of having the boosters crawl down our throats, and label you as a bad actor for not sitting him."

Swicegood turned and took another glance out of his window overlooking the field. He seemed to be considering this for a moment before turning around again, his eyes flashing with contempt like never before.

"No deal," he snarled.

Howser cursed as he turned around toward the door.

"You have no idea what you're doing!" Stinson bellowed. "Swicegood, your arrogance is going to drag down this program!"

Surprisingly, Jeff Swicegood let out a laugh at this. "Arrogance," he taunted Stinson. "Talk about hypocrisy."

Stinson, unaccustomed to pushback, leaned forward and slammed his hands down on Swicegood's desk.

"You better know," he growled, "what you're getting yourself into."

"I do," Swicegood responded, his own eyes still flashing with anger. "And you need to get the hell out of my office."

Stinson stormed out, with Howser trailing behind. When we were alone again, I glanced at my head coach.

"You sure you know what you're doing?"

Swicegood sat down in his desk chair and glanced at me. "I know what I'm doing."

"Why?" I asked him. "Why Jakobe? Why the commitment to him?"

Swicegood gave a faint chuckle. "Two reasons: One, it's my team. And two…" he paused and seemed to be searching within his soul for the answer. "I believe Jakobe."

"Over Katie?"

"Yes."

"Saying that out loud could get you in a ton of trouble nowadays, especially in a culture that emphasizes believing the victim."

Swicegood turned slightly in his office chair. "I'm confident in my decision…as well as my instincts."

"What does that mean?"

"I've been coaching a long time, Jayce," he said. "Long enough to be able to read people, especially my players, when it comes to lying versus telling the truth."

"And you think Jakobe's telling the truth?"

"Yes."

"You think Katie's lying."

Swicegood shrugged. "All I know is my reading of Jakobe Ackerman's given me no reason to think he's lying. And until that changes, he stays at quarterback."

I nodded.

"And Charlie Stinson can go to hell."

I arrived at my office at 6:15 Monday morning. Usually, the parking lot was empty by that time, and while it was not jam-packed at that early hour, there were signs that it would be soon.

A group of women had just gotten out of a passenger van and were putting together what looked like protest signs. They wore matching pink shirts, and their faces bore angry looks.

I could not hear everything they were saying, though I did make out the words "one of the coaches." Instinctively, I quickened my pace, wanting to avoid what I sensed was an ugly scene brewing.

"Excuse me?" came a shrill voice from behind me.

I slowed down. The worst thing I could do, I reasoned in that instant, was to dart away and make it look as though I was running.

Turning, I saw a woman in her mid-forties, not much older than me.

"Are you Jeff Swicegood?" she almost demanded.

"No," I answered. "I'm one of the assistant coaches."

"Did you have *any* say-so in whether or not Jakobe Ackerman played that game last week?"

"Who are you?" I asked.

"Never mind," she said, her tone of voice rising with each syllable. "Because we need to get to the bottom of why that predator was allowed to play when the university had a rape charge pending against him. Coach Swicegood needs to answer for this!"

Now I was ready to turn and run, appearances be damned.

"Coach, you bear the responsibility!" she was almost yelling now, as I opened the double door to our office building – inside the stadium - and rushed inside. Campus rules prohibited any type of demonstration inside university buildings, which was the only thing that kept that woman from following me inside.

I took the elevator up to the coaches' suite, got off, and noticed right away that I had a visitor standing outside the door to my cramped coordinator's office.

Darcy DeMarr greeted me with a "good morning" and a look that conveyed that it was anything but.

"What can I do for you, Darcy?"

She managed a grin. "I'm here to see what I can do for you... or maybe I should say what we can all do for each other."

"Come on in."

Moments later we were sitting in my office with Styrofoam cups of steaming coffee.

"We have Katie's statement," she told me.

"And?" I asked.

She took a sip of coffee. "Can't tell you the details. But it directly contradicts Jakobe's story, which we figured would happen. She says she remembers going upstairs with him that night, despite being drunk. Like I said, he denies it."

"Where is she?" I asked.

Darcy seemed confused. "Why?"

"Because," I began, "I care about her, and I want to know she's safe."

"She's safe."

"I don't suppose you can tell me where she's staying."

"I can't," Darcy began. "But I can tell you she's been moved out of her dorm and into a private residence."

"Private residence?" I asked, confused. "Whose residence?"

"Can't tell you."

I nodded. "Why come to me?" I asked.

"I tried Swicegood," she said. "He's hard to talk to, though. More pissed off about the bad publicity than what's happened here."

"He's pissed because someone leaked the story."

"As well he should be. Like it or not, though, public perception gets an unofficial vote in these things. Even if we find that Jakobe Ackerman has done no wrong, we'll all still take a beating in the press. 'He's done this before...now he's done it again...why isn't he being benched?'"

"Because Swicegood won't do it."

Darcy nodded as if she anticipated my reaction. "He still probably needs to sit until this thing clears; at the very least until my office has had a chance to exonerate him. And if we're able to do that—if we find that Katie's not being truthful or has her facts mixed up—then he can go back to playing."

"How long would that take?" I asked.

Darcy shrugged. "Long as it needs to, Jayce. Trust me, you don't want a black eye like this on your program.

There was noise coming from the parking lot; strange, unfamiliar noise that I was unaccustomed to hearing at this hour. Voices, getting louder; protesting voices.

Darcy heard it too. "We're expecting over a hundred women's groups by lunchtime. Angry groups. This thing has metastasized quicker than any protest-related issue that I've seen. And I was alive when Betty Friedan marched."

"What do we need to do?"

"Bench Ackerman," she retorted. "Do it today, so that the university doesn't take heat, not to mention lose financial support."

"It's a college campus," I told her. "A playground for groups that like to protest."

Darcy shot back. "Try telling that to the over twenty colleges in America that are facing financial shortfalls due to the support they've lost over incidents just like these."

"I can't bench a quarterback. I don't have that power."

"You're the offensive coordinator."

"Working for a guy who likes to control his team."

Darcy looked me in the eye. "Then tell your coach that if he wants to keep control of his team, he'd better listen to you."

"Not," Swicegood snapped as we jogged to the practice field that afternoon. The volume of the protests in the stadium parking lot had been climbing all day, and had reached what we hoped was a crescendo. As we moved along the fence that hugged the parking lot's edge, both of us could barely hear each other.

He continued, "I respect the hell out of Darcy DeMarr, but she doesn't get to dictate personnel decisions on the field."

"She's not dictating," I responded. "She's advising, which is her job."

"Yeah, well, I've got a job, too," Swicegood retorted.

I decided that was far enough. Swicegood's mood had been darkening progressively since Jakobe's story had gone public. We had ignored headlines, television, and social media, but the bad publicity was still making itself known. Our parking lot told the story.

Practice was spotty. Multiple forecasts were saying that Fall was going to be a hot one in our neck of the woods, and the players' sluggishness showed. Defensive players missed tackles, offensive linemen missed assignments, and Jakobe was feeling the pressure of both the starting job and everything else that swirled around him.

"How's your head?" I asked during one set where Connor was leading the second-team offense.

Jakobe stood next to me on the sideline. "Head's fine," he answered. "I'll be all right."

"You think so?"

"It's bullshit, but yeah," he said.

"Just gotta trust the process, Jakobe."

"Process is trying to eat me alive, man," he replied.

We were silent for a few moments while the second team kept practicing.

"You know I didn't touch her, right?" Jakobe asked, staring at me and causing my insides to burn. "You believe me?"

"I want to believe you," was all I could manage as a response.

Jakobe scoffed. "Yeah, and you also think I need to be sitting behind Connor from now on."

"Just until this thing dies down," I protested. "It's all coming from…"

"From Darcy DeMarr, I know," he interrupted. His tone was angry and subdued. "You think I don't see what's going on, Coach? Do you think I don't hear things? I know how close you are to Katie, and I know what the university's trying to do. They don't want the bad pub. The question is: do *you* see what's happening here? Do you see how y'all are being set up?"

"Set up?"

"Someone's clearly trying to hurt me, and hurt this program," he added. "They're using my past against me and trying to bring us all down."

My mind went back to the conversation with Swicegood in his office; how he seemed to think that someone had purposely leaked the story to the paper in Lexington when they ambushed him at the press conference.

"I hate it," he went on, staring out at the field. "I hate how you're branded for life in this world. I'd give anything to take back what happened at Louisville. I was stupid. But having someone pin it to me so that it never leaves me, and then using it to hurt my new team – my new family…including Katie – I can't think of a worse hurt."

I stayed late at the office that evening, finishing up some preparations for our next game; an away match-up against Dashford University in Missouri. It would be our toughest opponent yet.

I turned off my laptop, as well as my touch-screen, mounted above my desk, and got ready to leave.

I heard a door open in the hallway, followed by the sound of footsteps out in the darkened corridor. Figuring it was the evening custodial crew, I was surprised when I saw who had entered the top floor of our stadium offices.

Charlie Stinson stood at the end of the hallway and stared out of a window that overlooked the parking lot where, hours earlier, hundreds of women's groups had descended upon Yearwood State University.

He turned when he saw me.

"Coach Leonard," he intoned in that deep, oily voice of his.

"What do you need, Mr. Stinson?" I asked.

He turned from the window, hands in his pockets, and began ambling his tall, stately frame toward me.

"Rotary meeting earlier," he said. "Figured I'd swing by the campus on my way home."

I said nothing as I closed my office door and locked it.

"I like coming to this campus," he added, coming to a stop. "Always have. Some days more than others, but that doesn't change the fact that this campus will always be my home."

I nodded.

"Generations," he continued. "Generations of Stinsons have called Yearwood State home. And you know, walking around this campus; it's almost like walking through a family burial plot at a cemetery. All these buildings and facilities were built with Stinson money, bearing the Stinson name. Puts a lot of pressure on you, if you let it."

I nodded.

"But I wear that pressure as a badge of honor," he told me. "And as a responsibility. Guess that's what family money does for you. It's security, but it's also responsibility; making sure that not just you, but the next generation behind you, gets to succeed also."

"Is that why you're pushing to get Connor on the field as a starter?"

Stinson grinned a fatherly smile. "You're way more perceptive than your head coach, Leonard. That's for sure."

I said nothing.

"Truth is, I've got a lot of connections to this place," he went on. "But even so, that's not what I like about it the most." He stopped and looked me in the eye with a grin. "Do you know what I like most about this campus?"

I shook my head.

"It's peaceful," he said, folding his arms and leaning against the wall. "Yearwood State is a peaceful college campus. Or at least it used to be." He gestured with his head toward the window overlooking the parking lot. "Damn shame what happened out there earlier. The parking lot's a wreck; probably will take weeks to clean it all up."

"Probably so," I agreed.

"Of course," he continued, "it's nowhere near as big a shame as what happened to that poor girl, Katie."

"I agree."

"I've seen her with the team before," he added. "Sweet girl."

"She is."

"What happened to her should not have been allowed to happen," Stinson added. "But it's exactly the kind of thing that does happen when leadership fails."

"What do you mean?" I pressed.

Stinson grinned. "I think you know what I mean. Jeff Swicegood knew what he was getting with that Ackerman kid, and yet it didn't stop him from signing him and putting him in the spotlight where he doesn't belong."

"Jeff didn't cause Katie to be raped," I defended.

"Jeff also doesn't appreciate the value of this program enough to properly vet who gets to join it," Stinson snapped, his smile disappearing. "Hell, the truth of the matter is that part of it's not even his fault. Unlike you and me, he never went to college here."

"He loves the program."

"Not as much as we do," Stinson argued. "Not as much as we can. Here are the facts, Jayce: this program's been headed in a downward spiral for years, due to the failures of Jeff Swicegood. What's done is done, and the past can't be helped. The future, on the other hand…"

I glared at Charlie Stinson, whose gaze had softened as he kept his eyes on me.

"The future," he went on, "belongs to those of us who went to school here, and who care about the legacy and the direction of this program."

He stopped and gave me a large grin, but only with his mouth. His eyes still had a menacing glare to them.

"For my part, I love this university and this football team. And I don't want it to go down any farther than it already has."

I said nothing.

"Do you agree, Coach Leonard?"

I refused to make eye contact with those menacing eyes, but managed to say, "I agree."

"Good," Stinson affirmed, as he stepped forward and patted me on the shoulder. "That's what I was hoping you'd say."

CHAPTER 12

I got home that night, took off my pants, and crawled into bed exhausted.

Dixie, already asleep, stirred next to me as I burrowed under the covers.

"Did you eat?" she whispered.

"Not hungry," I answered.

I heard her sit up in bed. "You okay?"

"No."

She leaned over and rested her head on my chest.

"Are you still mad at me?" I asked her.

"For what?"

"You know for what," I replied.

She sighed. "No. I just want what's best for Katie. Only because I love and care about her as if she were really ours. You know that."

"Yeah."

"And I'm sorry if I was hard on you about it," she said. "I just got scared."

"I'm scared for her, too."

Both of us were silent for a moment.

"I heard about the protests," she said.

"It was wild out there today," I confirmed. "Hundreds of pissed-off women in our parking lot. Social media is even worse. You don't want to read some of the messages that mine and Jeff's pages got; not to mention the team's and the university's."

Dixie laughed softly. "At least you've only got one angry woman to deal with at home, right?"

I smiled at her through the darkness and put my arm around her shoulders, cradling her.

"Stinson stopped by the office earlier," I said after another minute.

"Charlie Stinson?"

"Yeah."

"What did he want?"

"Wants Swicegood out," I told her. "Blames him for what happened to Katie. Said if Jakobe had never been signed, none of this would have happened."

"Stinson's out of control."

Both of us lay there, neither of us caring about the hour, or how much sleep we were missing.

"I'm starting to hate football," I stated.

Dixie lifted her head, her eyes now adjusted to the dark, and looked at me.

"Don't say that."

"It's true," I affirmed. "I hate what it's become."

Dixie studied me for a moment.

"I remember watching you on the field during your first game as a starter," she said.

"High school?"

"Yeah."

"I think we lost that game," I tried to recall.

"I can't remember," Dixie said. "But I'll never forget watching you throw your first touchdown pass to Ahmad that night."

I smiled at the memory. Ahmad Floyd, one of my best friends from childhood, high school, and coaching, had caught my first touchdown pass in high school.

"You ran down the field and tackled him in the end zone afterward. Remember that?"

I laughed out loud. "God, I do remember that. He got up hobbling, too."

"Yeah, he did," Dixie giggled.

I marveled at the fact that we were now like two teenage kids lying in the dark and laughing.

"Faraday chewed my ass for it, too. 'Dammit, Jayce, if you hurt my best receiver, I'll run your ass till you puke next practice!'" I mimicked my former high school coach.

Dixie and I laughed again. When we had calmed down, she continued.

"Even though we weren't together at the time, and even though I wasn't a football fan then, I'll still never forget seeing you tackle Ahmad after that first touchdown throw," she said.

"Why is that?"

She locked eyes with me through the darkness. "Because it's the moment I remember realizing that football was your passion, Jayce. And by 'football,' I mean the sport, not the bullshit that you're having to swallow now."

I stroked her face, thankful that God had blessed me with this woman.

"Swallow the bullshit," she told me, touching my hand, "but remember why you're doing it."

"I love you."

"Love you."

She lay back on my chest and we were still for a moment.

"What are you thinking about now?" she asked.

"Sleep."

"Yeah right," she scoffed. "If you were thinking about sleep, you'd be asleep by now."

"You know me too well."

"So what were you thinking about?"

"Honestly," I answered, "I was thinking of Ahmad."

She laughed. "Guess my reminiscing is responsible for that, huh?"

"Maybe," I agreed. "Guess I was also just thinking of home, too."

"Yeah."

"I could use a trip back there."

Dixie sat up again. "A trip?"

"In the offseason, I mean."

"Homesickness?"

"Something like that," I told her.

Dixie said nothing. Through the darkness, I could barely see that she was nodding her head.

I put my arms around her as she lay on my chest. Within minutes, we were both asleep.

Dixie had a doctor's appointment the next morning, so I took Jamie to school. The drive to Yearwood High was a quiet one, between Jamie's sleepiness and my frustration over everything that was happening. I did not feel like talking, and so as Jamie nodded off while we drove, I just let my mind wander.

Mostly, I thought about Katie. We still had not heard from her, not seen her, and had only been told that she was working with Darcy's office and getting counseling of some kind. No word on whether she planned to stay at school or go home to Ohio or anywhere else. I prayed for her, and prayed for our program; that whatever nefarious elements were at work would be stopped.

"You okay, Dad?" Jamie interrupted my thoughts.

I glanced at him, surprised that he was awake.

"Yeah," I told him.

He grinned. "You're never this quiet."

Jamie had a point. Normally, he and I would be engaged in some manner of robust conversation, usually about football, as I took him to school. Sometimes the radio was on, tuned to a local sports news station, sometimes not. Either way, my car was never as quiet as it was today.

"Just a lot on my mind," I told him.

"About Jakobe."

"Mostly Katie," I clarified.

We drove on in silence for a few minutes.

"What's on your mind?" I asked him, eager to change the subject.

Jamie shrugged. "Just the game Friday night."

"Think you'll be ready?"

"Hope so," he answered. "The other team's got a sick defense."

"Yeah?" I looked at him.

"And they like to blitz their cornerbacks, who are fast."

"No kidding."

"Last team they played, their quarterback got hurt, because he didn't see the corner rushing him."

"Are you afraid that might happen to you?"

"Not really," Jamie clarified. "But we need to be ready."

"Always need to be ready," I said. "Especially against something you might not see coming."

Jamie nodded and stared ahead as if he were in thought. I wondered if the same lesson was sinking in for both of us at that moment.

Always need to be ready...especially against something you might not see coming.

"You'll make the right decision, Dad," Jamie said, reaching over and touching my arm. "You always do."

I smiled and tried to suppress the emotions I was feeling. "Thanks, son."

Two weeks later, by the time we finished playing Dashford University and Arlington College – two opponents that we faced on the road in Missouri and Arkansas, respectively – I was ready for a bye week and a road trip home.

Dashford beat us 20-9 and only sealed their victory in the final seconds of the game. In the first quarter, they jumped out to a 13-0 lead. But we rallied in the second when Jakobe scored our only touchdown on a designed quarterback run from 34 yards out. After that, we kicked off to them, and on the ensuing possession, our defense got a safety when Adalius Bennett sacked Dashford's quarterback in our end zone. Throughout the third quarter and most of the fourth, the score stayed as it was, 13-9.

With less than two minutes to go, our offense was driving. Jakobe completed five straight passes, to put us beyond the fifty-yard line. All we needed was a touchdown to win the game.

Then he took the snap, dropped back to pass, looked down-field, and threw a perfect swing pass out to Downtown Mathias Brown, our star running back. Downtown made for the sideline and was able to turn the corner. With the angle he had, he was going to get yardage, if not a touchdown.

However, he was also being chased by Dashford's fastest line-backer, who dove, punched the ball out of Downtown's grasp with his fist, and tackled him.

The ball spurted out and was caught on the fly by one of their safeties, who ran it back sixty-five yards for the game-sealing score.

We were angry and devastated at the way we had lost, but none more so than Jakobe. Even though Downtown's fumble had zero to do with him, his competitive fire—which had led us to pursue getting him to Yearwood in the first place—was on display. In the locker room, he was inconsolable and it became clear that he had been rattled by the loss, as well as everything else that was happening to him.

Jakobe was off all that next week during practice, and it showed when we took the field against Arlington College in Arkansas the following Saturday. They beat us by an even worse score: 31-7, and while Jakobe only threw one interception—along with a touchdown pass—he was hardly the dynamic leader and athlete that we knew he could be.

And the cries for benching him in favor of Connor Judd became louder.

"Let's take the week," Swicegood told me afterward. "Let him catch his breath, relax a little. Following week, we'll coach him up some more and see where his head is."

"Sounds good," I told him.

It didn't sound good to Charlie Stinson, who caught me as I was leaving the stadium late that night after the team bus had dropped us off following the Arlington game.

"Think Swicegood'll finally come to his senses?" he asked, walking alongside me as I made my way to my car.

"Not now, Charlie," I said, ready to be home.

Stinson, not accustomed to being spoken to in such a manner, stopped and nudged me so that I turned. "Connor's a better quarterback, better decision-maker, and everyone knows it."

"Everyone's also tired," I retorted. "And I'm not discussing this now."

"You ought to discuss it," Stinson pressed. "You owe it to your future as a potential head coach to discuss it."

For the first time, I looked up and studied his face. He wore an arrogant smirk.

"Remember, I'm a guy you want in your corner. Now's the time to make that move at quarterback, and put Connor in. You do that, I'll make it worth your while, Jayce."

"I've got to go," I told him.

"You think about what I said."

CHAPTER 13

Things did not get any better.

I got a call the next morning from Jim Gill saying that Mom had fallen at home after tripping on an uneven part of her living room carpet. She'd hit her head on the coffee table and momentarily lost consciousness.

Thankfully, she'd had her phone in her jeans pocket and was able to get it out and call the Gills once she regained consciousness. Jim and Jacqui had rushed over right away and tended to her. Other than bruising, there was no immediate reason for alarm, but that had not stopped the Gills from taking her to the urgent care facility in Lake Barrow to be evaluated as a precaution.

The doctors also found nothing wrong with her condition. She'd have a nasty bruise right above her left eye and some swelling, but nothing serious beyond that.

Still, it was a reminder that Mom's living room carpet needed replacement, and had been for years. Previously, it had been just an eyesore – discoloration, permanent stains, and the like. However, it was obvious that there were ridges and other bunchings popping up in the carpet that were not there before, and were now posing serious trip hazards, especially for someone with a walker. And as such, getting rid of the carpet became a priority.

Over the phone, Jim Gill and I struck a quick bargain. If I would come home during Yearwood State's bye week and remove Mom's old living room carpet, he would foot the bill for new hardwood flooring to be put in.

In short, Mom would soon have a safer space to move around in, and I would be taking the trip home that I'd been wanting (and probably needing).

Both Dixie and Jamie were supportive and were even insistent that I go home and tend to Mom.

"We'll video chat during Jamie's game," Dixie assured me. "This way you won't miss it."

And so, on that same morning, I packed a couple of bags, threw them in the car, and went back inside to say goodbye before leaving for Lake Barrow.

Milo had spent the previous night at our house, and he and Jamie were at the breakfast table when I came back in through the front door.

I walked into the kitchen where Dixie was standing over a frying pan full of sizzling bacon. Even though I had eaten already, I could not resist grabbing another slice before I got on the road.

"Stop, you!" she swatted my hand with a grin. "It's for the boys. Well, Jamie, at least."

I chuckled. "Milo, you want some bacon, too?"

Milo glanced up, and I noticed that while his face bore the same cheerful look as it often did, the usual energy was missing and he looked a little paler than normal.

"No thanks," he answered. "Not really hungry."

"He must not have slept well last night," Dixie told me, her brow furrowing slightly as she studied Milo. "It's funny, though, because both of them were snoring when I checked in on them last night."

"Probably just misses his bed," I told her.

Dixie nodded. "Maybe."

"Guess I'd better hit the road," I told her, leaning in for a kiss.

Our lips brushed, and I then went to the table and told both Jamie and Milo goodbye.

"Milo, you keep an eye on things for me, okay?" I said. "You're the man of the house."

"Really?" Jamie asked in mock indignation, looking up from his game console. "What am I?"

"A video game addict who can't be trusted," I teased, causing Jamie to grab a wadded-up napkin and fling it at me.

"Mustang pride, Coach!" Milo beamed, perking up and giving me a fist bump.

"Mustang pride!" I smiled at him.

Swicegood agreed that my trip home was best suited for those first few days—Monday through Wednesday—of our bye week. This would give me plenty of time to tend to Mom and get her house situated so that I could get back in time for the weekend. We would then scout our next opponent—Carthage University in Mississippi—and spend the subsequent week prepping for them.

I stopped for gas at a station near campus and got out. When I had filled up, I headed inside the building to get in line and pay.

I was staring ahead and letting my mind wander when I heard the door's entry bell ding. Glancing over, I had to do a double-take.

Katie Corvin was standing right in front of me.

She noticed me as I noticed her and froze when our eyes met, almost as if I had caught her red-handed in a place she should not have been.

"Katie…" I mouthed, almost reflexively.

She usually was dressed in stylish T-shirts and jean shorts. But today, as she stood in the doorway of that gas station, even though the morning temperature was already north of eighty, she had on baggy sweatpants and a large button-down flannel shirt that seemed to swallow her whole. She also wore no make-up, and her hair was frizzed and unkempt.

In short, she was nothing like the ebullient and upbeat Katie I had last seen following the Marquis State game.

She turned and darted out the door as quickly as she had come in.

I went after her; had to go after her.

Bolting into the parking lot, I spotted her as she hastened to her car, which was parked in a spot around the corner of the building.

"Katie!" I called.

"Leave me alone!" I heard her say, angrily but not loudly.

"Wait, I just want to check..."

"I SAID GO AWAY!" she yelled.

This got the attention of several other patrons in the lot, who turned and saw me—a middle-aged man—running after a young, college-age vulnerable-looking woman.

So, I stopped, glancing around as I backed up a few feet. Then, turning my eyes back to her, I said, "Katie, I've been worried sick about you. We all have. And I just wanted to make sure you were okay."

"Do I look okay?" she retorted, a look of resigned anger flashing in her hollow eyes.

"Katie," I pressed, "whatever it is, whatever you're going through..."

"You have no idea what I'm going through!"

I had to regroup quickly. She was on the defensive and was not backing down. "Whatever it is, let us help you," I said to her.

"I'm getting help," she said. "I'm doing what I need to do."

"Okay."

"No!" she almost screamed. "It's not okay, and you have no idea."

With that, she got into her car, cranked the engine, and peeled out of the parking lot.

Within seconds, she was gone again.

I thought about her the entire drive.

She was on my mind as I crossed the state line from Kentucky into Tennessee and passed the exit for Portland and Orlinda. She stayed on my mind as I reached Nashville only a short drive later, and interchanged onto I-24, going toward Murfreesboro. I fought to distract myself by focusing on the rolling hills and picturesque farmland that dotted the landscape of that drive; terrain I had practically memorized throughout my college days as I had trekked back and forth between Lake Barrow and Yearwood. But it was to no avail.

I prayed for her as I reached Chattanooga and headed farther south, into Georgia and toward the great city of Atlanta. By the time I had made it through town and fought with the traffic, I was exhausted.

Katie—and her welfare—had dominated my thoughts and prayers.

Before I knew it, the sky was dark and I was in Florida. I felt myself mashing the gas pedal a little harder as I trekked toward Gainesville, the last major town before the Lake Barrow exit.

I stopped for fuel near Micanopy and bought a coffee, trying desperately to stay awake for the last few miles I had to drive.

As I filled up my car and sipped my coffee, I tried to empty my mind and keep Katie off of it.

Soon, a car pulled up to the pump next to me. When it parked, the doors opened and out stepped a little girl of about six. She wore a costume consisting of a multi-colored leotard and a pair of butterfly wings suspended from her shoulders with elastic loops.

Her brown hair was pulled back in a ponytail and she smiled at me as she stood by the car.

"Want to hear me sing?" she asked me without preface.

I turned, looking to make sure there was no one else around to whom she could have been speaking.

"Do I want to hear you sing?" I repeated, clarifying.

"Macy, leave that man alone," scolded her father, who had gotten out of the car and begun activating the gas pump. "You don't talk to strangers." Then, turning to me, he said, "Sorry, pal."

I waved to him, signaling that it was no problem.

I looked back at the girl, whose face now bore a disappointed look. Maybe it was that look, or maybe it was my fatigue from having driven all day, or maybe it was just Katie. Whatever it was, I somehow—in that moment—saw her wings and leotard disappear and saw her instead wearing the same thing that Katie had been wearing earlier that day; baggy jeans and an oversized dress shirt.

I blinked and she was back in her costume again.

"I'd love to hear you sing," I blurted before I could even stop myself.

Her father looked up at me in surprise, glanced at his daughter, and gave a faint grin. "You sure?"

"Absolutely."

The father hesitated a little, then said, "Okay then. Sing for him, Mace."

I listened as this little girl then launched into a rendition of "Jesus Loves The Little Children" right there on the spot. She sang her heart out, and when she had finished, I clapped for her.

"That was beautiful," I told her. "Good job, Macy."

"It's Macy Katherine," she informed me.

Katherine...Katie. I suddenly needed to leave.

I said a hasty goodbye, paid for my gas, and drove off moments later.

Heading the rest of the way home, I still thought of Katie.

But for the first time that day, after hearing that little girl sing, I now felt confident that all the prayers I had said for Katie Corvin would somehow be answered someday.

Lake Barrow is nestled between the Florida cities of Gainesville and Ocala. Known for its agricultural production, it had been my hometown since Rex Leonard, my stepfather who had adopted me, had moved my mother and me there right after they married in 1985. Life had been great up until Rex's death three years later when he had fallen off of a condominium roof that he had been finishing in Orlando. Ten years after that, my mother had suffered an accident when a car hit her.

In the wake of both of those incidents, we had been surrounded by the love and care that only a small town like Lake Barrow can provide. For all of its foibles and imperfections—things you normally associate with a small town like ours—my hometown took us in during those trying times and will forever be the place I call "home" as a result.

It was late at night when I drove into town, but not even the darkness could conceal the fact that Lake Barrow, Florida had not changed a bit since I had last moved from there in early 2010. The town square, with its stately courthouse, city hall, and small, boutique-style buildings that housed several of the town's small business mainstays was still the same. Just beyond the square lay the newer strip which was populated by several of the more modern franchise chains; restaurants and other larger-scale stores. Nestled right in the middle of that hodgepodge of modernity was Jim Gill Automotive, founded by Jim Gill's grandfather, and currently run by Matt Danforth.

Just around the corner from there was Sims County High School, where I had made a name for myself on the football field both as a player and as a coach. And it was there, as I drove past, that I spotted the first noticeable difference.

"Frank Beezer Parkway" was the new name for "Sims School Way," the name of the road that had taken me to school for four years of my life.

I laughed to myself, remembering that Mom had once told me—after I moved away years earlier—about the street name change.

Frank Beezer, I smiled to myself.

He had been the groundskeeper for the school's athletic facilities, including our football field, for as long as I could remember…right up until his retirement in 2012. And he had died the very next year, right after football season.

"Beezer," as he was known, had always been possessed of an almost spouse-like affection for all things Sims County athletics, and particularly when it came to how he took care of the football field. We loved him, even if his devotion to the fields got him in trouble at times; like the time Sims County and Barton City got into a brawl following the game. Beezer had almost attacked a player from the opposing team for "disrespecting his field" and had needed to be tackled to keep it from happening.

I chuckled at the memory, unpleasant as it had been at the time.

I reckon it will always be memories like those that keep me coming back to Lake Barrow, and calling it "my home."

It was well after midnight when I had pulled into the driveway, and Mom was already asleep. So, I crashed and did not even bother to change my clothes.

The smell of pancakes and eggs woke me up the next morning. This was a good thing since I had wanted to get up early and not sleep late.

The only bad part about this was that mom was doing the cooking. Even though her physical condition was okay, she still moved sluggishly—and always would—because of her bad hip. Thus, I hurried into the kitchen as soon as I realized that she was making breakfast.

"Let me help," I told her as I darted for the stove and offered to take over.

She smiled at me. "You can help," she said, "by sitting down and eating some of this…or all of it."

"How are you feeling?" I pressed.

"Fine," she waved me off. "No need for you, or anyone, to fret."

"I'll fret less when we've gotten that carpet up," I told her. Then I proceeded to give her a run-down of my plan for the living room.

I would spend the first part of the day running errands; doing odds and ends for Mom and maybe picking up a few tools I would need to pull up the carpet. This would kill time until the afternoon when my help arrived. My friend, Ahmad Floyd, the current head coach at Sims County, will be coming to assist with moving furniture and taking up the carpet. Additionally, Jim was dispatching Matt Danforth from the dealership to come help as well.

"Sounds like a plan," Mom affirmed. "You'll need your strength first, though. Eat."

"Smells delicious," I said, grabbing a spatula and taking a few pancakes off of a griddle nearby.

"More food than I've cooked in a while, I can promise you that," she chuckled as she emptied a panful of scrambled eggs into a large plate.

"Just imagine if Jamie and Milo were with me," I told her, sitting down with a glass of orange juice.

"I sure wish they were," she almost lamented, keeping her eyes on the stove. "I miss the rest of my family."

"They miss you too."

"That Milo," she went on with a smile, "you all sure have taken him in."

I nodded and took a sip. "He's a sweet kid."

"I'll never forget watching him run across that field," she told me.

"Nor will I."

My mind went back to that afternoon; before the quarterback controversy, and before things had really begun taking a downward turn. It all must have shown up in my face as Mom sat down with the egg plate.

"Well," she said, putting down the eggs and picking up her coffee cup with a grin, "I would ask 'what's wrong', but based on the headlines I've read coming out of Yearwood, and from talking to Dixie, I can probably guess."

I gave a faint chuckle. "At least I don't have to rehash the whole thing with you."

"Anything new?"

I shook my head as I began fixing both of our plates. "Jakobe's investigation is still ongoing, and until we know something, Swicegood doesn't want to bench him."

Mom nodded. "What about Katie?"

I ate a bite of food and took a deep breath. Then I told Mom about running into Katie at the gas station on my way out of town the previous day. Mom listened and kept watching me with a sympathetic gaze. When I had finished, she just shook her head.

"She's hurting," Mom stated.

I just nodded. "And I don't know how to help her."

Mom took a sip of coffee and seemed to think it over. "Just be available to her and dependable for her," she told me. "Availability and dependability."

"Your two greatest abilities," I finished with a smile, remembering one of the greatest lessons she had taught me growing up.

CHAPTER 14

"What's up, J-man?" Ahmad beamed at me that afternoon, as I greeted him and let him in through Mom's front door.

I smiled and tried to think of how many times Ahmad, accompanied by Jamie Gill and Deke Hudson, had walked through that door when we were growing up. I had lost count, and as I turned and looked at Mom who was smiling and welcoming Ahmad, I wondered if she had any idea herself. Looking at him, it was hard for me to believe that Ahmad Floyd, who had been reluctant to start coaching with me years earlier, was now the head coach at our alma mater.

He looked the part of a head coach, too, having come straight from practice that afternoon and dressed in athletic shorts and a "Sims County Spartan" t-shirt. Like me, he was now middle-aged, but Ahmad Floyd carried himself with the same energetic, athletic intensity that had always characterized him.

"Thanks for doing this," I told him.

"Aw, it's no problem," he scoffed. Turning to Mom, he asked, "How you doin', Ms. Cheryl?"

"Just fine, Ahmad," she answered, as they hugged. "A little embarrassed at being so clumsy, but I'm sure I'll make it."

"Of course, you will," he told her. "We're gonna take care of you."

She smiled and thanked him.

"Matt should be here soon," I told him. "After that, we can get going."

Ahmad laughed. "Man, I still can't believe Matt Danforth," he said. "Working for Jim Gill Automotive, *and* he's coming over here to help you move furniture and carpet."

"It is weird," I agreed, as we sat down on the sofa and waited for Matt. I offered Ahmad something to drink, which he declined. Mom left us and headed to the kitchen.

"Man, I remember Sims County-Barton City back when we first started coaching that first season," Ahmad said with a laugh.

"God, I've been trying to forget that game ever since it happened," I cringed.

Ahmad shook his head. "Morgan Danforth gets hurt, after Jordan Gill late-hits him from behind and tears up his knee. Then a riot almost breaks out on the field. And then, here comes Matt charging the field and trying to get Jordan for hurting his little brother."

I just shook my head as Ahmad recounted the painful memory.

"And yet, here we are today," Ahmad said, holding up his hands. "Everybody's getting along finally. God's good."

I nodded and agreed. "How's the team?" I asked.

At this, Ahmad's expression changed, and I almost felt bad for changing the subject.

"We're all right," he said without much conviction. "Only one win, but we're fighting."

"Heard you guys lost a bunch of seniors from last year."

"Yeah, but it ain't just that," Ahmad continued. He paused and seemed to be trying to put into words what he wanted to say. "It's the mentality."

"How do you mean?"

"You're a coach, Jayce," Ahmad replied. "So, you probably see it every day yourself. Is there any real loyalty to your program up where you are?"

I thought for a moment. "I guess with some guys, there is."

"Some guys," Ahmad repeated. "The majority, though?"

I shrugged. "Most guys do what they need to do for themselves," I said. "A lot of it playing time and giving themselves a shot to make it to the pros."

"That's my point," Ahmad affirmed. "And it's even worse at the high school level. I had one guy last year who transferred here from Barton City midway through the season. He played two games with us and got benched because of grades right before what would have been his third game. Right after I told him he was benched, he left my office and transferred to Benford."

Ahmad laughed, but there was nothing light-hearted about it. "Crazy, man."

"Makes for a rough time," I told him.

"Too rough," he said.

I studied him. "Too rough?"

Ahmad shook his head. "Last week I got a call from an old associate of mine from back in the day. You remember the dude I was working for right before you convinced me to coach with you?"

"Yeah," I said. "Electronics, right."

"That's the one. Since I left, they've done well for themselves; selling mostly high-end electronics to government outfits and such. Big payoff."

I studied him. "You thinking of going back?"

"I'm starting to," he affirmed. "Don't get me wrong. I love coaching and love the kids, but it's not what it used to be. You know I almost got fired from the district last year for making the boys run soul sprints?"

"You're kidding me."

Ahmad shook his head. "It used to be that this job was about wins and losses and helping kids. Nowadays, it's fifty percent that, and the other fifty is making sure your ass is covered before you make any decision about anything. Shit's crazy."

I shook my head.

"It's not even that I want to quit, but it's just that I don't know if I'm the guy for this job anymore."

I just sat there listening.

"And if I'm not," he went on, looking at me, "then the only thing to do is step aside and make room for whoever that person is."

I couldn't argue with that.

The sound of a car engine pulling into Mom's driveway interrupted our conversation.

"Matt's here."

"Let's get started," Ahmad said, getting up from the sofa. He rose slowly, and for the first time that afternoon, Ahmad Floyd looked older than I'd ever seen him look.

"Praying things work out for you," I offered.

"Thanks, Jayce."

Matt Danforth had bounced around the country after high school trying to find himself, as the cliché went. Along the way, he'd found plenty of alcohol, dead-end jobs and relationships, and several wasted years.

Despite all of that, he looked good and was doing well as a senior manager at Gill Automotive. Like most of us, he had gained some weight around the torso and face since high school but was dressed in a fashionable pair of sweatpants and a long-sleeve t-shirt.

"What's going on, Leonard," he greeted me with a faint smile. I shook his hand, returned the greeting, and thanked him for coming.

"Don't thank me," he dismissed. "Jim threatened to fire me and start a new war with my family if I didn't oblige him on this."

I laughed as we went inside.

Matt and Ahmad exchanged cordial greetings, which was a far cry from our playing days at Sims County, when the two could not stand each other. I remembered how Ahmad had almost quit the team our senior year due to having to run receiver routes for Matt and put up with his attitude. Not only was Matt a sub-par quarterback, but he'd also had arguably the worst demeanor of anyone else on the team, all of which had led to him being benched in favor of me during that same season.

It was evident, though, that time had healed those old wounds, and the three of us began working right away. We moved Mom's furniture out of the living room and either put the pieces into another room in the house, or outside on the porch or front lawn. Her furniture was mostly easy to move, and I was surprised at how simple the operation was, even though there were only three of us working.

The carpet was next. Using pliers and box cutters, we had the whole thing detached and cut into strips within an hour. Following this, Ahmad took care of the carpet padding, and Matt finished things off by unfastening the tack strips. Once those tasks were completed, we put the furniture back where it had been, ready to be moved once more when Jim's flooring crew came in and started working.

"Here's to bare concrete floors, but no more trip hazards," I toasted my two friends as we sat on Mom's porch and drank cold beers that I had picked up at the store earlier.

"Here's to no more brawls on Soul Rasheed Field," Matt quipped, "that result in me getting my ass kicked."

Ahmad and I guffawed loudly at this.

"Man, I wish my guys played intensely enough to want to fight somebody," Ahmad stated.

"I actually saw the Barton City game a few weeks ago," Matt said to Ahmad. "Not gonna lie, they looked pretty lethargic."

"Speak your mind, bro," Ahmad said with a grin.

"I'm saying it in love," Matt clarified with a chuckle.

"I catch myself saying it without love sometimes," Ahmad added.

We sat there taking in the cool evening breeze. Autumn—or Florida's version of it—was finally making its presence felt. Soon, Ahmad had to leave. When he was gone, Matt and I sat on the porch finishing our beers.

"How's the family?" I asked him.

"All good."

"Got one of your own?"

He shook his head. "Not yet. Been seeing this girl from Daytona for a while. We'll see how it goes."

I nodded.

"How about Morgan?"

"He's great. Lives up in Jacksonville with his family. Works at a church."

I smiled.

Matt continued, "Says his knee injury – the one Jordan caused - was the best thing that could have happened to him. Says he never would have found Jesus and gone into ministry if it hadn't happened."

"Youth pastor, right?"

"College and young adults."

"Good for him," I affirmed. "Your parents moved there, too, right?"

"To be closer to the grandkids, yeah," he grinned.

"Kinda left you holding the bag down here in good ol' Lake Barrow."

Matt scoffed. "Wasn't much of a bag to hold once Dad sold the business, and the new guy took the property company elsewhere in the state."

"You get to see them much? Your folks?"

"Mostly holidays."

"Why stick around here, then?"

He shrugged and thought about his answer. "Guess it's just home. Doesn't matter how many folks come and go. I grew up here...grew a lot from being here, as a person."

I nodded.

"It's funny. Me losing the job at QB our senior year, followed by everything that happened after that, and ending with the fight on the field when you coached that first year. I guess it all needed to happen to help us come to our senses."

"Maybe so."

"You taught me a lot, Jayce," Matt said. "Even if you didn't mean to."

For some reason, my mind went to the issues that I had left behind up in Yearwood. Before I could stop myself, I said, "I wish I could teach Charlie Stinson a lesson."

"Who?"

I chuckled at myself for having said it out loud, almost unwittingly. Then I explained to Matt what had been happening at the university. He listened with interest and seemed taken aback at the situation with Katie and Jakobe.

"Sounds like a lot," Matt observed.

"Yeah."

"That Charlie guy sounds like a real peach."

"Rotten peach," I corrected.

He laughed. "You've got a real tendency for running into those types and having to deal with them."

"Regrettably so."

We sat watching the sun set toward the west.

"Guess I'm not the ideal person to give you advice," Matt finally said, "but I do know that Lake Barrow's in the improved state that it's in largely because of you, Jayce."

"Soul deserves credit for that," I dismissed. "Not me."

"Both of you," he said.

"Truth is, I wish Soul was still here," I added. "He'd know what to do."

Matt nodded his head. "My brother's fond of saying that God gives and takes away," he told me, "like the Good Book says. Maybe that's the lesson for you here."

"What do you mean?"

"I guess I'm saying that Soul's gone, and that's a tragedy. But then maybe this hard time up in Kentucky that you're having is probably for the same reason as the one here in Lake Barrow all those years ago. Maybe you're struggling because you don't have Soul with you for this go-around. But that doesn't mean you don't have what you need to overcome this."

I stared off at the blackening sky and nodded my head.

"Just be yourself, Jayce," Matt said. "That's how you and Soul helped this town years ago, and it's probably how you'll get through this latest fiasco up in Yearwood."

"Thanks," I told Matt.

On Thursday morning, I packed my bags again and said goodbye to Mom before taking off. The flooring crew had come the previous day and—thanks to the smallish size of Mom's living room space—had finished the job in an afternoon, including the time it had taken for them to move the furniture around.

"You drive safely," Mom said as she hugged me on the driveway. "And thank you for helping with my new floor!"

"You deserve it," I told her. "And you need it."

"Well, I don't want to bust my ass again," she quipped, causing both of us to laugh. "Or my head for that matter."

I left and was headed out of town, but decided to drive by the old high school before hitting the county line.

Once I arrived, I figured I might as well go inside since I was there. After making my way in, I spoke briefly to the front desk receptionist, a younger lady that I had never seen before, and asked to speak to the principal if she was in.

The principal was. Moments later, Mikayla Hudson emerged from a doorway behind the front office. She beamed when she saw me.

"Get over here, boy!" she exclaimed, coming toward me.

We embraced and I was thankful to see my old friend. In addition to being the younger sister of Deke Hudson, Mikayla had distinguished herself as a track and field star, first at Sims County, and then at the University of Florida. Then she had come home to Lake Barrow around the same time I had, where she had taught English and coached track.

Now, she was making history as the first black, female principal that Sims County had ever hired.

"It's good to see you," I told her after she had escorted me back to her office.

"Likewise," she said, easing her athletic frame into a seat. She wore a stylish white dress shirt, elegant jewelry, and a pair of fashionable black dress pants. Her long hair was curled and pulled back into a ponytail, which accented her high cheekbones. She had always been beautiful, which was undoubtedly one reason why my late friend Soul Rasheed had been attracted to her.

"How's school?"

"Doing fine," she said with a smile. "Always testing, it seems, but we're making our way; the Spartan way."

I grinned, remembering our school's old motto.

"' How are *you?*' is the question," she asked me.

"Doing well," I told her.

"I'm surprised to see you here," she said. "No game this week?"

"No game, and a family emergency," I answered, before filling her in on the details of Mom's fall and her new living room floor."

"Wow," Mikayla said. "I'm glad your mom is okay."

"Thanks."

"A lot of excitement," she observed, "especially with ol' Danforth coming in to help."

We both laughed.

"Yeah, I was a little surprised."

"I was shocked when Jim hired him," she said. "But I was glad to see it, just the same."

"Me too."

We made small talk from there; families, Deke, parents, et cetera. At one point my cell phone rang. I reached into my pocket, felt around for the volume button, and pressed it, silencing the tone.

"Any new boyfriends?" I asked her with a grin.

Mikayla scowled at me. It was the same look she'd given me during childhood whenever I would kid her. "In Lake Barrow, Jayce?"

"Ahmad's still single."

"Oh, my goodness!" she exclaimed in an exasperated tone which made me laugh. "Don't even go there."

"I won't," I assured her. "Fact is, coaching probably keeps him too busy for any sort of love life."

"Yeah, and his keeping us in trouble with the district probably keeps me from having my love life," she quipped.

I nodded. "He told me he'd gotten in trouble with the district over making the boys run soul sprints."

Mikayla shook her head. "Bless his heart, he's doing the best he can…but he's just an old-school guy in a new age. Heck, you know what I'm talking about; both of you guys were coached by Faraday."

"Faraday," I said, thinking back to my old high school coach. "He was a hard-nose."

"You could be too," Mikayla chided. "But then you had Soul to help balance you out."

I could not help but notice the slight softening of her demeanor when she said his name.

"Yeah," I told her. "He sure did."

Both of us were silent for a moment.

"I miss him," she finally said.

I just nodded, at a loss of what to say. Soul's death had perhaps been harder on Mikayla than it had been on anyone else.

"I miss him too," I affirmed.

Mikayla had been looking away for a moment. When she turned to look at me again, she smiled. "Of course, this whole town misses you as well, Jayce," she said. "And you know you're always welcome home when you want to come back."

I sat there for a moment watching her; the same little tomboyish girl who had tried to follow me and her brother around whenever we played as kids. She was now a glass ceiling-shattering education professional with her own life, achievements, and life goals. I was proud of Mikayla Hudson and glad to know her.

"Tested and tried," I told her.

"Spartan pride!" she finished.

I walked out of my high school alma mater, ready to return to Yearwood, but decided to take a short tour of my old campus before I left. As I walked around the main building toward the rear, my route took me to where the old field house stood, which is where my old office was located.

Suddenly, I felt faint. Maybe this wasn't such a good idea.

Sure enough, the dizzy feeling gave way to chills and cold sweats.

Good grief…this many years later.

It was the shooting. That cataclysmic event that had helped define and shape not just my life, but the lives of so many…in more ways than I could even count.

It was how I had lost Soul Rasheed.

All I could do was stare at the building that I had been walking through—on my way to meet with Andrew Starr, our then-principal—when the first shots rang out.

Inside that same building was the classroom where Soul Rasheed had been killed; while trying to protect Jordan Gill and another female student who had taken shelter in the classroom's closet. The gunman had followed them into the room, and Soul had gone in after him; determined to preserve Jordan's life by any means necessary, even if it meant sacrificing his own.

Which it had.

I brushed away a tear, unaware that I had even been crying, and decided to get out of there. Hometowns hold memories good and bad, and I had now experienced both. It was time to go home.

I walked back around the main building. As I approached my car, I reached into my pocket for my keys, and my fingers brushed against my cell phone. I then remembered that someone had tried to call while I was in with Mikayla.

I pulled out the phone and was surprised to see that I had both a missed call and a text message from Quinn Howser.

Keying into my phone, I opened the message, read it, and then felt my blood run ice cold.

Jayce, we need to talk. I just fired Swicegood. You're now the interim coach of the team.– Q.H.

I forgot all about Lake Barrow, the memories, the shooting, all of it.

Stunned, I got into my car, managed to crank it, and began heading toward the interstate.

Chapter 15

"I'm okay, Jayce," Jeff Swicegood told me over the phone an hour later, "and I'm not surprised. Howser's been pressured for weeks to make this decision, and we both know he handles pressure like a cheap deck chair."

I listened as my car neared the Georgia state line.

"I'm sorry, Jeff," I told him.

"Don't be," he told me. "At least you're getting a promotion out of this."

"Which I didn't want; certainly not this way."

"Nobody does," Swicegood agreed. "But that's the profession we've chosen."

"You sure you're all right?"

"Yeah," he said, without hesitation. "I know what I did was right, even if others don't agree with me. I don't think Jakobe did what he was accused of. Public opinion doesn't agree with me, and that's a problem in our line of work."

I could not disagree.

"You hang tough, Jayce," he told me, just before we hung up. "You're one of the good ones. Just don't let the crowd noise change that."

The Next Day

Quinn Howser's office was in an adjacent building near the stadium, and I hustled to it after parking my car at the university the next day.

In less than twenty-four hours, I had received a flurry of texts, phone calls, and news updates about the firing. By the time I pulled into my driveway, I had used what little energy I had left to give Dixie a quick kiss goodnight and fall into bed with my clothes still on.

As I jogged through campus that morning, I prayed that no one would recognize me.

Sometimes God's answer to prayers is a resounding "no," and sometimes he answers in the negative with prowling journalists.

"Coach Leonard!" shouted a parasitic reporter who had been lurking near Howser's office building as I ambled up. "Can you speak to the decision by the university to fire Jeff Swicegood?"

I stiff-armed him with a "no comment" as I entered through the glass doorway, but the volume of his voice had attracted other students who were making their way across campus. They began moving in my direction as well; curious to hear what the latest and greatest was regarding our football program.

I made a beeline inside the building and brisked my way up the stairs to the second story where Howser's office was located.

I nodded to the secretary, grunted a good morning, and stated my business.

"He's waiting for you," she informed me. "Go right in."

The office was spacious and ornate, yet understatedly so. Howser had the obligatory ego wall situated directly behind his desk, complete with his few accolades as a Yearwood State athlete, and the many more which he had garnered as a sports administrator over the years.

His desk was large, and put enough comfortable space between himself and whoever was in his office. As I entered, he rose and gestured to a leather chair, which I sat down into.

"Jayce, I'm going to get right to the point," he told me. "We're in a tight spot."

I nodded.

He continued, "And it's not just because of Jeff's firing, but because of the reason why. And as you know, it's the Jakobe situation."

"And the feminist groups."

"Right, but even more than that," he said. "We've got high-profile donors getting ready to pull out over this, Jayce. They've seen the news. They read the headlines; they know the narrative by heart. 'Yearwood State is a safe haven for rapists.' All of it. We can't afford the fallout."

"That's why Jeff was fired."

"Basically," Howser admitted. "It's an optics game, Jayce, every bit as much as it's an X's and O's game. In a game like that, you have to listen to reason."

I gave a cynical smirk. "Are we changing Charlie Stinson's name to 'Reason,' then?"

"Don't give me that crap," Howser bristled. "If Stinson said anything, it was probably because he saw the writing on the wall, too. He's a pain in the ass, but he's our pain in the ass, and as it so happens, he's also the pain in the ass that keeps the lifeblood pumping through this place. You know this as well as I do."

I studied him. "I'm assuming you didn't drag me over here just to sing Charlie Stinson's praises."

"Of course not," he answered. "I brought you here to make it official; you're the head coach until further notice. And you need to bench Jakobe Ackerman until further notice."

"So, we're following Stinson's marching orders."

"Until this shit storm, we're in dies down, yeah."

I sighed and rose from the chair. Howser seemed to read me.

"I don't like it any more than you do," he tried to commiserate. "I'm not on that practice field every day, but I know what you're up against. Connor Judd's nowhere near the athlete that Jakobe is, but until we can navigate this whole mess, Judd's your guy under center."

"And if I don't start him?"

Howser glared at me. "I've been doing this job for most of my professional life. And I've never had to fire two coaches in the same week." He paused and glared at me. "Don't force me to make history."

I turned and started to leave.

"Congratulations on your promotion," he said, as I opened the door. "And make the right call."

Like any team that's faced the turmoil of losing their coach midway through the season, the guys were dejected at the news of Swicegood's firing. We broke the news to them the next day right before practice.

Swicegood was usually decked out in Mustang colors but had showed up that day wearing a pair of slacks and a plain windbreaker—a subtle, gentle confirmation to everyone that he was no longer affiliated with the program.

"How are you feeling?" I asked him, as we stood side by side. All around us, the players were beginning to file onto the field and huddle up, waiting for us to begin.

"Like I've been punched in the dick," he answered.

I gave him a pat on the shoulder.

Once the players stopped arriving, we figured we had most of the team, and decided to start.

Swicegood went first and gave his final remarks to the team he had coached for sixteen seasons. It was an emotional moment, and even though he was wearing the same pair of sunglasses he usually wore, there was no mistaking the breaking in his voice, and the few tears he wiped away. He wished the guys the best, talked about the memories made, even called a few players out.

Deon Flowers with the longest punt return in school history. Downtown Brown with the fumble on the one-yard line in that one game, but he redeemed himself later with a sixty-yard scoring jaunt.

Adalius Bennett with what would have been a scoop-and-score on a fumble recovery, but he got the ball stripped out of his hand right before he crossed the goal line and gave it back to our opponent.

There was laughter and a few tears, and on several occasions, anger at the fact that Swicegood was being let go.

Finally, Jeff Swicegood finished his final good-bye to the Year-wood State Mustangs, and was given a send-off with a massive group hug from the team and plenty of well-wishes. Each player came by to shake his hand and give him an individual hug of their own.

When it was over, he turned to leave and shook my hand for what I figured might be the last time…for at least a while.

"Team's yours, Jayce," he said in a shaky voice. "Mustang pride."

"Mustang pride," I told him.

I waited for him to leave before giving my own address to my new team.

Stability is important in a situation like that. And so when I started to speak, one of the first things I wanted to do was give the guys the standard line of, "nothing's changing/it's business as usual/full speed ahead."

And yet I knew just how untrue a statement like that would be. Truth was, the quarterback situation was still up in the air. Despite the missive from Howser, I still wanted Jakobe at quarterback. Connor was a talented guy, but he could not carry the team the way Jakobe could.

And so I held off on telling the guys that it would be business as usual.

Of course, my plan to hold back could never stop the rumor mill.

"Coach, what about QB?" Deon Flowers, our receiver, asked.

"Yeah, I heard we're gonna have to go with Connor now," Downtown Mathias Brown added.

"Let me worry about that," I answered. "You'll know something when we know."

At that moment, I glanced up and saw that Charlie Stinson had made his way onto the practice field and was standing near the back of the group watching me address the team. At that moment, I could not decide whether I hated him more for what had happened to Swicegood, or because he felt he could take the liberty of letting himself onto the field whenever he damn well pleased.

I also wondered if he had run into Swicegood as the two of them were coming and going from the field. I almost chuckled at the thought.

Nevertheless, I wrapped up my remarks and dismissed the guys, who were all wearing street clothes and would be back for practice later.

I wanted to avoid Stinson, but had no such luck.

"Congratulations, Coach Leonard!" he called out as I started to walk past him.

"Save your congratulations."

I did not stop, but he kept pace with me. Stinson was wearing a navy business suit with no tie and wire-rimmed sunglasses. No doubt he'd come from a business engagement of some kind and was in a relaxed state as he checked up on what he considered "his" team.

"Don't be like that, Jayce," he said. "And you shouldn't feel too bad about Jeff either. He had it coming."

"I'm sure he did."

He chuckled. "You really don't like me, do you?"

"Definitely have a laundry list of things I'd rather do than associate with you."

"Fair enough," he conceded. "So, I'll make this quick. Connor should be your starter. You know it, I know it, and Quinn Howser definitely seems to know it."

I increased my pace.

"You're a great coach, Jayce," Stinson called out as I strode away from him. "Use this opportunity to your advantage, and don't jeopardize it."

Dixie texted me after practice that afternoon and said to meet her at Tootsie's for dinner before Jamie's game that night.

Milo's accompanying us to Jamie's games had become almost as commonplace as the games themselves, which is why I was surprised to see only Dixie sitting there waiting for me as she read a menu.

"Where's Milo?" I asked her, after we had greeted each other with a kiss.

"At home," she said, the worry lines deepening in her face. "Still sick."

I sat down, worried.

Dixie sighed. "His grandma said she thinks he's feeling fine, but then she also mentioned possibly needing to take him to the doctor, or maybe even the ER."

"Should we go see about him?"

"His grandma assured me that she has it all under control, and I don't want to be overly intrusive."

"You seem worried."

"I'm a mom."

I tried to focus on the menu.

We ordered our food. When it arrived, both of us ate in silence for most of the meal. Truth was, we were both eager to get out the door and make it to the game before kickoff.

"You seem worried yourself," she said, taking a bite of salad. "Which is strange, given that you just got the promotion that most assistant coaches dream about."

I smiled at the irony, because she was right. We should have been celebrating there at Tootsie's that night. But instead, we both felt tired; me especially.

"Just the week," I said. "Start scouting for Carthage tomorrow."

"Are they good?"

"They will be against us, if I end up starting Connor at quarterback."

Dixie reached over and touched my arm. She knew the headlines, same as everyone. The difference was that she had a front-row seat to how the entire situation was affecting me, combined with the politics in the athletic department and boosters.

"We'll be all right," she said. "Whatever you decide to do."

I nodded and went on eating my steak sandwich. When I looked up again, there were tears in Dixie's eyes. I reached for her hand. She took mine.

"I was just thinking…remembering," she told me.

"About what?"

"About coming here with Jamie, Milo, and Katie that one time."

I smiled. "The shout-out from Deke," I said.

"Seems like forever ago," she told me, wiping her eyes with a napkin. "Before things got so crazy."

"I hear you," I nodded.

"Guess it just seems like longer ago than it really is."

Jamie's team suffered their first loss of the season against the number three team in the state. If that wasn't bad enough, Jamie had his worst game of the season, throwing three interceptions and no touchdown passes. In fact, his only real contribution to the game was a one-yard scramble for a touchdown late in the fourth quarter.

The final score was 35-13.

Beyond that, the next week was a whirlwind as we got ready to play Carthage on the road. Even though I had coached with Jeff Swicegood and had seen up close how demanding his job could be, I was nowhere near prepared for the rigors and responsibilities that a head coach had to endure. There were meetings, and lots of them. There were responsibilities to take care of, mostly related to travel arrangements for our team. And of course, there was preparation on the field as well.

There was not a single night during that first week where I did not have to be awakened by Dixie in the middle of the night after crashing in the bed with my clothes on. Despite my exhaustion, she always managed to get me roused long enough to get a shower and change into some variation of sleepwear before passing out in bed again.

All of it led up to the next Friday as we boarded the team bus to head for the airport, where a small jet would fly us to Tupelo,

Mississippi. From there, we'd take another charter bus that would transport us the rest of the way to Carthage University to face our next opponent.

It would be my first game—and first test—as a collegiate head coach.

I figured in the air was as good a place as any to break the news to Jakobe and Connor.

We coaches were sitting in first class, while the players occupied the coach section. Sticking my head out beyond the curtain, I made eye contact with both of them and motioned for them to come join me.

The two of them arrived at the same time; both wearing jackets and ties with plain, white button-down shirts.

"Have a seat," I told them, gesturing to two empty first class berths that were across from me. Jakobe sat directly across, and Connor sat to his left.

"Guys, you know why I called you back here, so I'll get right to it," I said.

I glanced at both of them. They were composed, but it was clear that they both wanted me to come out with it.

Taking a deep breath, I said, "Connor, it's your ballgame today."

Connor wasn't usually a smiler, but he was now grinning.

Jakobe gave a slight frown and looked downward.

"Here's the important thing," I said to them. "Both of you guys are still part of this team. This decision does not change that. So, I expect you to play and practice accordingly from here on out."

"Yes sir," Connor said.

Jakobe said nothing.

"You guys can head back to your seats," I told them.

Connor rose briskly and walked back into coach. Moments later I heard sounds of whooping and hollering as he was congratulated by his teammates, after having told them the news.

Jakobe just sat there.

"Something on your mind, Jakobe?" I asked him.

"Just a question," he said, looking up at me, a pained expression on his face. "Do you think Swicegood would have benched me?"

I was caught off guard by his inquiry and had no answer.

Finally, I said, "I don't think that matters now, Jakobe."

"It matters to me, Coach."

"Then the best answer I can give you is that I don't know what Swicegood would have done."

It was a pat answer with no conviction and Jakobe saw right through it.

"You know I didn't do anything," he said in a soft voice. "But it's okay."

I studied him.

He went on. "It's politics and it's sports. People love you and then they stop loving you. I just wasn't sure which side of the political aisle you were on."

He got up and went back to his seat, and I watched him go, at a loss as to how I was supposed to feel in that moment.

For as long as I'll ever coach, I'm sure I'll always remember the Carthage game as one of the most memorable ones of my career.

It was memorable because the guys pulled together to win it, 23-17.

It was memorable because Connor took us downfield with under five minutes remaining, and scored the winning touchdown himself on a scramble out of the pocket.

It was memorable because of our defense—which had been getting run over all game. They kept Carthage's offense out of the end zone, even though Carthage drove the length of the field late in the game.

It was memorable because we then stopped them on the goal line after four downs.

It was memorable, because it was my first win as a college head coach.

And it was memorable because of the events that happened immediately afterward.

In the locker room, the team celebrated like never before. Loud music blared, impromptu dance-offs materialized, and even Jakobe—who had been subdued but supportive throughout the game—seemed to get more upbeat as the celebration went on.

The team even managed to get me in the middle of the circle as the dancing was happening. Camera phones came out, and I was soon making a fool of myself amidst all of the merriment.

When it was over, Connor came up and hugged me.

"That was awesome, Coach."

"Not as awesome as watching you carry the team, kid," I told him. He grinned.

"Thanks for the opportunity!" he beamed. "I appreciate it."

I could not help but smile. And in the back of my mind, I was reminded of how different Connor was from his uncle and, presumably, from the rest of the Stinson side of his family. He was a humble kid who just wanted to play ball, no matter the politics behind how he got his shot.

I was happy for him.

Gradually, we got all of our equipment, personal belongings, and personnel together and were getting ready to leave. After a quick shower, I changed back into the suit I had worn on the trip, and gathered my pocket items: wallet, keys, and cell phone.

Looking at my phone, I noticed that I had four missed calls, all from Dixie.

Stepping out into the hallway, I called her back.

She answered after the first ring.

"Jayce," I heard her say in a shaky, soft voice.

"What's wrong?" I was alarmed.

Silence.

"Babe?"

Muffled sobs.

"You need to get home as soon as possible," she said, her voice breaking. "It's Milo. He's in the hospital."

"What?"

"Get home immediately," she almost wailed. "He's not expected to make it through tonight."

Chapter 16

What should have been a celebratory trip home turned out to be an angst-ridden and secluded nightmare for me instead.

I sat in my own seat, away from everyone else, and tried to rest…tried to pray…anything to put my mind at ease, even though I knew that was impossible. All I could think about was Milo.

My son's best friend.

Our "second son."

The kid who had changed all of our lives simply by being himself.

There had to be a mistake. He wasn't feeling well the last time I saw him, but surely, he could not have been as sick as he was now. Surely his fragile heart was not failing him.

Surely, he wasn't dying.

We landed, and I put one of my assistant coaches in charge of getting the team and equipment settled, so that I could bolt off to Yearwood Memorial Hospital.

Driving across town, I cursed red lights and prayed like I never had before. When I reached the hospital parking lot, I swerved into the first empty spot I saw, jumped out, and ran inside.

Dixie had texted me the number of the room in ICU and I wasted no time finding it once I got inside the building.

I turned the corner, and slowed to a walk when I saw Dixie and Jamie standing outside of a room.

Jamie saw me first, and made eye contact.

Tears. Red eyes.

Oh, God, no.

Dixie's face was a similar mess. She wore no makeup, otherwise it would have been running down her face.

Jamie leaned with his back against a wall, and did not move. But Dixie came toward me and was falling apart with each step.

Could it be true?

"Jayce…" she began.

I said nothing, but locked her with my eyes, even as I felt hot tears coming to them.

"Jayce…"

"Tell me," I finally managed to say.

Dixie lost what remained of her composure. "We lost him," she cried. "We lost our Milo."

I felt myself go numb, even as the tears began flowing freely and involuntarily. Dixie and I embraced, and Jamie came over, choking on his own sobs, and hugged us both.

There we stood, in the middle of that drab, white, sanitized hospital with raw emotions pouring out of us.

It was minutes—that seemed like hours—before we finally pulled apart from one another and were able to converse again.

"What..?" I asked Dixie, trying to formulate a sentence. "What happened?"

"It was his heart," she said, wiping away another tear. "Same condition he'd had since birth."

I shook my head and stared at the ground.

"He was wanting to see you," Jamie said, his face contorting as fresh sobs welled up from within him. "Wanted to see one last game. Wished he could have been there to watch y'all today."

"It was a hell of a game," I said, putting my arm around him for support. My other one was draped over Dixie as we walked in the direction of Milo's room. "He would have been proud."

We stopped in front of the hospital room, the door to which was closed, and held onto each other one more time.

"Is he in there still?"

Dixie nodded. "His grandmother's with him."

"How is she?"

Dixie shrugged. "Like the rest of us," she answered. "But holding it together."

I glanced at the door, wanting to go in; knowing that I needed to see Milo, but terrified just the same.

"Go," Dixie said, reading me. "It's okay."

I walked in, not knowing what to expect.

Seated next to the bed was Milo's grandmother, a frail woman in her sixties who looked older than she was. She had kind eyes and hair pulled back into a gray bun. She smiled weakly at me as I entered.

"Hello, Coach," she said, rising from the bedside where she had been holding her grandson's hand.

I nodded to her and encouraged her to not get up. She did so anyway, walked over, and embraced me.

As I turned my head, I got my first glimpse of Milo Crenshaw's lifeless body. He lay there in a hospital gown, his lower body covered by a bedsheet. If not for the lack of movement in his chest—which was not readily noticeable—anyone who saw him would have thought he was just taking a nap.

My mind went back to seeing Soul at the morgue right after he was killed years ago. He had looked peaceful...just as Milo did now.

"I want to thank you," Milo's grandmother said to me, gently turning my face so that we were looking at each other. "For all you did for my Milo."

I felt my eyes welling with tears again. "Our Milo," I corrected her, before I could stop myself. "And he did more for us than we ever could have for him."

She gave me a faint smile. "All he ever talked about in the last week was that touchdown run," she told me, with a forlorn chuckle. "How he got to be a star for a day, and be a Mustang." She paused and glanced up at me. "You gave him that. You, Jamie, and your family...and the team."

I nodded in affirmation, grateful.

"I know it's tough right now," she said. "I read the headlines, and hear all about the terrible things that have been happening at Yearwood State. But I can only hope that as you're working through all of that, that you'll remember my Milo; and especially what your program and your team...and your family...all meant to him."

"Yes, ma'am."

She let go of me and I left her, walking over closer to the bed. Standing next to Milo, I watched him resting peacefully, without a care in the world now—not that he had ever been one to let cares of this world affect him. He lay there, almost as if in a dream somehow.

As I watched him, I closed my eyes and remembered; the sleepovers, watching him with Jamie, seeing his face as he chowed down at Tootsie's during the many outings on which he had accompanied us.

Then I saw in my mind's eye the one image of him that I knew I would never forget: the sight of him running stiltedly across Mustang Field for a touchdown as the crowd roared for him.

Milo's funeral was held on Thursday of that next week in the mid-afternoon.

I ended practice early that day, so that the guys could have time to clean up and get to the church on time. The team practically insisted that we do it this way, not that their insistence was needed. It was a secret to no one that Milo Crenshaw had been—and would always be—a member of our Mustang family. Keeping our players from attending his funeral would have likely led to a mutiny of some kind against me as a coach.

And so, I knew that the funeral would be well-attended. What I did not expect was the massive number of people who showed up. When I got there later that afternoon, I was sure that I had somehow ended up at the wrong location, even though I knew full well that I had arrived at the church where Milo and his grandmother worshiped each Sunday.

I pulled into the parking lot, being careful to navigate around the dozens of people walking through it. That was when I began to see a handful of my players walking together, several of whom had carpooled.

I was simply amazed at the number of lives Milo had touched.

My astonishment continued as I made my way inside, found my seat next to Dixie and Jamie near the front of the sanctuary, and waited for the service to begin. Milo's closed casket was situated right in front of the stage directly before the pulpit, where the minister and those sharing words of remembrance about Milo, would speak. Next to the casket was a framed, enlarged portrait of a smiling Milo; his school photo from the year before.

The service began and the youth minister of the church—Milo's youth pastor—stood up and asked everyone to stand. Then the pianist led off with a rendition of "Amazing Grace." When it was over, we all sat back down and the youth pastor began speaking.

Milo Dewitt Crenshaw, born June 7, 2004, passed from this life on October 12, 2019 into an eternity with Jesus Christ, his Lord and Savior. He leaves behind his devoted grandmother, Jessie Nettles, and a host of extended family and friends, all of whom were touched by Milo's life in some positive way.

He went on for several moments, and then turned it back over to the pianist, who played a medley of some of Milo's favorite songs. I did not recognize many of them; in fact, the only one I remember recognizing is, "You've Got a Friend In Me," from the movie "Toy Story."

Appropriate, since no one who knew Milo likely ever had as faithful a friend.

Afterward, it was time for more testimonies. Several of Milo's teachers, past and present, spoke of the sweet-natured kid he'd been, and what a joy he always was to have in class. These were followed by members of the community; Denvis McBride got up and spoke about Milo, as did Jeff Swicegood – who had agreed to speak at the funeral, despite all that had happened.

Then it was our players' turn. Many of them got up and spoke, and all of them mentioned Milo's now-famous touchdown run. But there were other memories as well; day-to-day remembrances such as his being around the team, helping Katie hand out water to the players, high-fiving the guys when they did something good, and heck, just being there.

There were tears and laughter.

Soon, it was Jamie's time to pay tribute to his friend. He had been preparing his words all week, and I prayed in that moment that he would do well. What did that even mean? I'm still not sure.

All I know is that God gave me a "yes" answer that day.

"I'm Jamie Leonard," my son began timidly, as he stood behind the church's pulpit.

Watching my son, who resembled me in that moment as he stood on the stage wearing a dark suit and tie, it took me back to two funerals: Soul's and that of my other best friend, Jamie Gill. On both of those occasions, I'd needed a moment to find myself, find my voice, and muster the wherewithal to say what I needed to say. My son, like me, now appeared to be in the same predicament.

"I was Milo's best friend," he went on. "We hung out together quite a bit over the past several years, and I guess that's how we got to be so close."

He paused and seemed to clear his throat.

"But it wasn't always like that," he paused. "When I first moved here a couple of years ago, I got pretty involved in sports around here, just like I've always been involved in sports. My dad's a coach, so we've moved a lot. And I guess sports were always my one constant thing wherever we went. We'd get somewhere and I'd go join the teams, whatever sport season it was. And that's how I made my friends.

"When I got here, though, I went out for sports, made friends like I always do, but then something was different. There was suddenly this kid who I had never met before...never met anyone like him. And his name was Milo Crenshaw." Jamie stopped and grinned, almost as if remembering seeing Milo for the first time. "He wouldn't leave me alone at first, and it kind of got to be annoying."

He paused again as people in the congregation began chuckling.

"Milo could always be stubborn that way, though," Jamie continued. "And he was definitely stubborn with me. He kept hanging around, wanting me to do stuff with him, and for a while, I refused him. I wouldn't hang out with him. I was too busy with sports, too busy with my new friends. You name it.

"But over time, I began to see that Milo was a lot like me. We liked a lot of the same foods, a lot of the same video games, same movies, you name it. And I guess what really got me to like Milo in the early going was how good he was at video games. He was one of these kids who just knew all the shortcuts, all the hacks, and all the ways to succeed that I never could figure out. It sounds pretty dumb and shallow, but that's how it was. Milo showed me how to win at video games, and that's how we really became friends."

Jamie paused again, and seemed to be collecting himself.

"But what deepened our friendship was not him showing me how to win at video games, but showing me how to win at life. And the only reason I know that today is because Milo…more than anyone else…saw something in me besides a jock. I mean if you think about it, how would a jock and a kid like Milo end up hanging out and being such good friends? Honestly, it was all Milo. He helped me see that, even though sports was—and still is—important to me, there's more to me than being an athlete. He showed me that I've got more to offer the world than just my arm, or my athletic ability, or anything else. He made me a better person, and I'll always thank him for that.

"And I'll miss him…" he glanced down at the closed casket directly in front of him. "I'll miss you, Milo."

Jaime left the stage and came back down. As I suspected, he had been holding himself together so that he could get through his speech. Now that it was over, he collapsed into the pew right next to Dixie, buried his face in her shoulder, and began crying.

At that point there was no holding back the tears for any of the three of us.

The graveside service for Milo was just as poignant, though nowhere near as elaborate. The youth minister read some scripture, and offered a few prayers, followed by words of comfort to Milo's grandmother.

It was a crisp autumn afternoon, and the leaves were starting to change color on the few trees that dotted the landscape of the cemetery.

Once the service was over, people began filing out and away from the grave site.

Soon, we were left sitting there under the tent with Milo's grandmother and a few other folks who were talking in soft conversations. Dixie and I were somewhat ready to leave, but Jamie was not, and so we decided to let his needs guide us as we sat there and waited.

Jamie, for his part, sat by Milo's grandmother and just stared at the casket, which would soon be lowered to its final resting place in the ground. Both of us sat on either side of him and just waited.

After about ten minutes, Jamie finally stood up, walked over to the casket, and gently caressed the mahogany. His voice was subdued, but I heard him utter ever so quietly, "Mustang Pride."

Mustang Pride...Spartan Pride. My memory raced back in time again to the two funerals of my best friends, Soul and Jamie.

Jamie rejoined Dixie and me, as we stood up and began to make our departure from the grave site.

As I turned to go, I noticed for the first time a young lady who had been sitting behind us. At first I did not recognize her; the cropped, dark hair, thin frame, makeup-less face, and long, black dress were as unfamiliar to me as if she had been a stranger.

But this was no stranger.

"Katie?!" Dixie almost exclaimed, recognizing her before I could.

Katie Corvin managed a faint smile at us before she stood up. She and Dixie exchanged a soft hug, and Jamie smiled and said hello, which she returned.

She said nothing to me.

"We weren't sure if…" Dixie began, struggling for the right words.

"…I wasn't going to miss this," Katie responded softly. "Milo meant too much."

Dixie smiled at her, and we stood there for a moment, not sure what to say next. Katie had cleaned up well, but still looked as gaunt as she had the day I had seen her at the gas station. She had lost weight, even though her figure had already been lithe to begin with, and it was most evident in her hollow cheekbones. Her eyes, once bright and cheerful, now appeared heavy. She had also cut her hair and dyed it a darker color—auburn-reddish, and a far cry from the blonde locks that had always helped us recognize her.

"I was hoping to talk to you," she said to Dixie. "You and Coach. Can we go somewhere?"

Dixie glanced at me, as if wondering what to say next. Jamie just stood there, his expression difficult to read; somewhere between confusion and the lingering quiet sadness from the funeral.

"Sure," Dixie answered.

A sense of relief seemed to come over Katie.

"Why don't we go to our house, then?" Dixie said. "Would that be okay?"

"Sure," she uttered.

We turned to walk toward the car, unsure of where Katie was even parked, though she knew the way to our house and would likely not have to follow us.

"I want to tell you the truth," she suddenly blurted as we walked.

Dixie and I turned. "The truth?" I asked.

"The truth," Katie said, "about what happened that night at the frat party."

Dixie and I kept our eyes on her.

"I think you should know that you were lied to," she said, her sentences now coming out in short, rapid-fire bursts. "Jakobe never raped me."

CHAPTER 17

A half hour later, the three of us—Katie, Dixie, and me—sat at our kitchen table. Jamie, exhausted from the day's events, had gone upstairs to take a nap.

At the table, Katie sat staring at a cup of coffee that Dixie had fixed for her and thought about how to begin. Dixie and I waited, occasionally watching Katie, but trying not to stare and make things even more uncomfortable than they already were.

"Whenever you're ready," Dixie told her.

"We're listening," I added.

Katie took a deep breath, sipped her coffee, and then straightened up in her seat.

"Like I said, Jakobe did not rape me," she began. Then she hesitated once more, as if the words were fighting to get out of her, but something unseen would not let them escape.

"It was Connor Judd," she stated.

I felt the room begin to spin as the news hit me.

"That party," she continued, "it was insane. I had never drank that much in my entire life. Growing up, it was kind of frowned upon, and besides, my parents needed me at home; to work, to make money. Didn't leave much time for partying.

She paused.

"But I drank that night. And I paid for it by nearly passing out downstairs. It was stupid. I had always been a good girl, good kid; always avoided those kinds of parties, even in high school." She paused and sipped her coffee again. "I guess I just wanted to see what all the fuss was about; getting drunk and also fitting in with the crowd. Joining a sorority was always a pipe dream of mine, too, I guess."

Dixie and I just nodded, and encouraged her to go on.

"The next morning, I woke up." She paused here and almost seemed to be choking back vomit. "And Connor was next to me in the bed. He's always been a nice enough guy to me, but never my type. And I'd even told him that before when he asked me out one time. We talked, and most of those conversations ended with him wanting a date of some kind."

"'Of some kind'?" I asked.

Katie shook her head. "Call it feminine instinct," she said. "But I always got the vibe from him that it was about sex with him."

Dixie nodded.

I sat across from her and rubbed my forehead. Connor Judd. The wholesome kid—whose uncle, granted, was a prick. Could he really have done this?

Katie seemed to sense my skepticism. "He's not who you think he is, Coach; and he's not who he puts himself out there to be," she stated. "Not only that, I'm not the only girl he's done this to."

This shocked me, and again, Katie saw it in my face.

"He's gotten away with it before, and for one very specific reason."

At this, I lowered my eyes, looked at the table, and cursed Charlie Stinson under my breath.

"Yeah," Katie affirmed. "His uncle's last name reaches farther than most people even realize. I guess whenever Connor has gotten in trouble before, along comes Uncle Charlie to clean up the mess with his cash and influence."

"Tell us more," Dixie encouraged. "Go on."

"Like I said, Connor was there next to me in the bed when I woke up. I start to freak out over what I thought happened, and so I sat up—a little too quickly. Not a good idea when you're hungover. And that's when Connor woke up. He jumped out of bed and said something like, 'Oh shit, I should have been out already.' I guess that was his plan; to be gone before I woke up so that I wouldn't suspect him at all, since I probably wouldn't remember.

"Then I asked him the obvious question, 'what happened?' He immediately says, 'nothing happened.' But of course I don't believe him. So I asked him, point blank, 'did we have sex?' and he said, 'yes, but you can't tell anyone, because I'll get in trouble.' And that's when it hit me."

"What hit you?" I asked.

"That Connor had raped me. I had been too drunk to consent, too incapacitated to say 'no,' and he had taken advantage of me anyway."

"What happened next?" Dixie asked.

"Connor starts getting dressed quickly. I'm sitting there trying to process everything, trying to come to terms with the fact that I've now become a statistic, like so many other girls and women." She paused and collected herself. "And at the same time, I'm getting angry; just furious at the fact that he's done this to me. It sounds strange even to say now, since I was so damn hungover, but in that moment, it's like the anger gave me clarity."

"What'd you do next?" I asked.

"I reached down to the floor, grabbed the pair of jeans I had worn, found my phone, and took a picture of Connor as he was getting dressed...for proof."

She managed a faint smile at this, proud of her own cunning and guile. Dixie and I smiled back at her.

Then, just as quickly, her smile disappeared. "That was when Connor flipped out," she said. "I honestly thought I was going to get beat up on top of the rape I had just gotten. He called me all kinds of nasty names; slut, whore, sneak, you name it. He said he would come after me with everything he and his family had if I told anyone. He tried to grab my phone, but I wouldn't let him have it. And I guess that's when he realized how loud things were getting, which caused him to panic."

She paused again, sipped, and seemed to be collecting herself.

"So he finished getting dressed, and ran out. But I remember he looked both ways down the upstairs hallway to make sure no one saw him."

"What did you do then?" Dixie asked.

"I got dressed and left," she answered. "Believe it or not, despite how angry I felt, I was scared, and ashamed, and in no hurry to expose him right then and there. At that moment, I just wanted to get the hell out of that house and never come back. I was feeling terrible, and all I really wanted at that moment was to talk to someone."

"Who did you talk to?" Dixie asked.

"Darcy DeMarr," she answered.

"Did you file a report?" I asked.

"No, not right then," Katie stated. "She asked me if I wanted to, and I said no. I was so scared, I didn't even say Connor's name, or state that he'd done it. Because all I really wanted to do was tell my story, and just have someone listen. But looking back, maybe that's what I should have done."

"It's ok," Dixie tried to soothe.

"Why is that what you should have done?" I asked.

Katie's face registered a bitter grimace. "Because of what happened after I left Darcy's office," she said. "I went back to my dorm, and the next thing I knew, Charlie Stinson was knocking on my door."

"Shit," Dixie said out loud, without realizing it.

"How did he even know where you lived?" I almost demanded.

"I told you," Katie answered, without missing a beat. "Until this incident, I had no idea just how much influence that man has over not just the athletics here, but the university. He gives money, which opens doors for him and puts power in his hand that no one else has; including having access to student records." She paused and took a deep breath before continuing. "So he came over to my dorm. I let him in, and he starts out by saying that he just wants to check on me, make sure I'm okay, et cetera. Apparently, Connor had given him his version of what had happened. So Charlie then went into a spiel about Connor; 'he was wrong for what he did,' 'he ought to have his ass whipped,' 'he's really sorry,' and on and on. Then he asks me if I'm planning to open a case with the university. And I told him I was thinking about it."

Katie paused again, and seemed to be struggling with her emotions.

"Then what did he say?" I asked.

Katie looked at me with tears in her eyes. "He said he thought it was a good idea," she answered. "But then he asked me how I would like to have my tuition paid off, my bills taken care of, and to not have to worry about money again while I was at Yearwood State."

"What?!" Dixie was flabbergasted.

"In exchange for what?" I asked.

Katie was brushing away tears with her dress sleeve, but they were falling faster than she could wipe. Dixie got up, fetched a box of tissues from the kitchen counter, and brought it to her.

"In exchange for telling a different story than the one that happened," she sobbed. "A story that would basically set Jakobe up to take the fall, once I filed a report accusing him instead of Connor."

"God," I whispered.

"I guess Connor also told him about my financial situation, needing money, all of it," she wept. "Once he had that information, he had a way to get Connor off the hook as well as finally get him into the starting job at quarterback. He also had a way to use Jakobe's background from Louisville to make him into the scapegoat he needed."

"So," Dixie said, trying to clarify everything. "He was going to pay you money to cover your tuition in exchange for pointing the finger at Jakobe instead of Connor, and saying that Jakobe raped you."

"Yeah."

"I don't get it," I told her. "How many witnesses would have seen you and Connor go upstairs together, instead of you and Jakobe?"

"According to Charlie, Connor had told him that we didn't go upstairs together. And Jakobe had gone upstairs with another girl some time before that, which put him in my vicinity at around that time."

I rubbed my temples.

"As for everyone else," she went on, "it was a party. Most everyone was too drunk to have seen, much less even remembered or cared, what went on upstairs."

"What about the picture?" I asked.

At this, Katie pulled out her phone, opened it, and within seconds had handed it to me so that I could see the photo she had taken of Connor. I almost had to stifle a laugh as I looked at an image of my starting quarterback struggling with his jeans, an indignant look on his face as he realized his photo was being taken.

I started to hand the phone to Dixie. "I don't want to see it," she waved me off in a bitter tone.

So I gave the phone back to Katie.

"Charlie made me delete it," she said. "Right there in his presence." Then she gave a faint chuckle. "Old people are funny, though. They look down on younger folks without realizing that we're the generation that can operate technology better than they can. Charlie's visit was a good example. I deleted the photo, but not before I quickly saved it to a separate folder when he wasn't looking."

"Smart thinking," Dixie told her.

For my part, I was struggling. Even though she had an incriminating photo of Connor that seemed to put him in the room with her after the rape, a part of me could not help wonder if she was making this whole thing up.

And then I hated myself right away for even thinking it. I fought to dismiss the thought as soon as I had it. On top of that, another notion came right on its heels.

Why in God's name, I mused, *would she be making this whole thing up in order to take on Charlie Stinson?* This was the first reason why I ultimately decided to believe Katie.

But secondly, and most importantly, I looked at Katie Corvin. This damaged young woman from Ohio, who had come from nothing, and whose parents had no means to put her through school, and who had taken out what would prove to be crippling loans, making her ripe for predation from the likes of Charlie Stinson; she had changed. She had been a peppy, upbeat, energetic force for our team and our university. And all of that was gone. Everything that had once made her "Katie" had disappeared. She was now a hollowed-out version of herself, devoid of any sense of self to speak of; all of her own self was pressed down by the force of rich and powerful men.

It's strange, but in that moment, I thought of my mother. After Rex had died, Mom had lived as a single woman. As such, she had endured on many occasions the ill treatment of predatory men; scumbags who stalked her, followed her into stores, came after her at work, and made her feel as nothing more than a piece of cheap meat. She tried to keep it from me, but I remember hearing her talk to friends about it, and had picked up on the bitter, hollow look in her face that I now saw in Katie.

This, I decided, was why I would believe her.

"Why not go to the authorities," I spoke up in righteous indignation, "especially if you have proof of…"

"Jayce!" Dixie snapped.

Katie's face dropped, almost in shame. Right away, I felt like an asshole…a noble, well-intentioned asshole, but an asshole just the same.

"I was humiliated," Katie said. "And scared. And to be honest, Charlie's offer sounded like a way out of it for me."

She was now fighting with her emotions once more, and her face crumpled into a deep, bitter frown. Tears followed.

"I hurt Jakobe," she sobbed, breaking down. "All I wanted was for it all to be over; the aftermath of the rape, the memories of it, the money problems I was having. I was blinded, and I was wrong."

Dixie got up first and went to her. I soon followed. We both put our arms around her.

"You've got nothing to be ashamed of," I said.

"You're the victim here," Dixie affirmed.

There we sat, at our table, both my wife and I flanking Katie Corvin, whom we both embraced…whom we both loved like a daughter more in that moment than at any other time we'd known her.

As such, I began to feel within myself something unfamiliar. Having had only a biological son, I had never—until that moment—known the kind of singular protective instinct that only dads of daughters can have. Katie had been wronged not once, but twice. First, by the soon-to-be-ex-quarterback of the Yearwood State Mustangs whose ass I was about to promptly kick off of the team in the next twenty-four hours. And secondly, by his manipulative tyrant of an uncle, who would get his—if I had anything to say about it—in short order following that.

Katie was still crying. "I had to make this right," she wailed. "I have to make this right; for Jakobe, but mostly for Milo."

"What do you mean?" Dixie asked, brushing away tears.

Katie shook her head. "Thinking about him this past week," she said. "Thinking about who he was; the ways in which he just loved people; loved our university, loved our football team. Everything about his existence was just...unblemished." She paused and began crying again. "How did everything get so fucked up?"

We loved on her some more, letting her cry.

"We'll make it right," I told her, feeling a rare combination of compassion and anger boil within me. "All of us...together."

CHAPTER 18

I stood by the entry gate to the practice field the next day... waiting.

One by one, the players came through and headed to warm-ups on the practice field. It was the day after the funeral, Friday, and one day before our next game against Bethel Trinitarian College, out of Bethlehem, Kentucky. We were expecting a blowout win, especially with all of the heartache we were feeling in the wake of Milo's death, and were itching to take our frustration out on a weaker team.

As for my own personal frustration, I was itching to take it out on Connor Judd, whom I saw approaching the gate.

When he passed through, I grabbed him by the shoulder pad and stopped him.

"We need to talk."

"Yes, sir."

I love all of my players, but what I felt for Connor Judd at that moment was about as close as I'd ever come to feeling hatred for a player in my entire career. The way he said "yes, sir" pissed me off, and I could not tell at that moment if it was because I finally knew what he was like underneath that "wholesome boy" façade, or if I was just pissed at myself for letting him—and his damn uncle—lead me down the primrose path about him for so long. Either way, my blood was boiling.

"You're off the team," I told him simply.

Connor took a step back, almost staggering, as he absorbed the blow.

I had him back on his heels and was wasting no time. Pulling out my cell phone, I retrieved the photo that Katie had sent me right before she had left our house the previous day. Holding it up, I showed it to Connor.

"Where the hell did you get that?" he asked in a gaspy voice.

"Katie Corvin," I told him. "Evidently, your uncle wasn't tech savvy enough to make sure she *fully* deleted that photo of you covering up your rapist junk before you left the frat house bedroom."

"She's lying!" he yelled, causing a few of the players to look over our way.

"Someone's lying," I mock-agreed with him, "but it ain't Katie. Go to the locker room, take your shit off, and get out of my sight. You're off the team."

For the first time since I'd known him, I saw anger—real, genuine, explosive anger—come to the countenance of Connor Judd. His eyes blazed. Gone was the amicable, compliant, working-class-hero demeanor that I had become so used to, and which I had come to appreciate as a coach. Now, he looked at me with outright hatred.

"You ain't seen the last of me," he snarled, as he stormed back toward the locker room. As he exited the gate, he slammed his helmet onto the asphalt drive leading away from the field. The impact caused one of the helmet fastenings to shoot off from the shell and skitter across the pavement. The helmet shell itself rolled listlessly to a stop with the facemask only halfway attached now. Connor's shoulder pads followed suit, as he threw them down also and kept walking.

Good riddance, you bastard, I thought to myself as I watched him walk away.

What the hell have I done now? was my next thought.

"All right, Jakobe!"… *"Yeah!"*… *"We got our main QB back now!"*
The team's reaction to my announcement that Jakobe Ackerman was returning as the starting quarterback was overwhelmingly positive. For this reason, I found myself reluctant to break the next piece of news to them.

"Guys, there's something else," I announced. "I just want you to know that Connor Judd is no longer with the team."

"What?" "Man, what happened?" "Why we keep having signal-caller drama?"

"All I can tell you at this point is that it's disciplinary, and he's no longer with us. As of today, McHenry, you're second-team quarterback, right behind Jakobe."

Travis McHenry was a redshirt freshman who had never taken a snap. He was a lanky kid with a decent arm, but nowhere near the athleticism of Jakobe—or Connor for that matter. Thus, Connor's departure, while necessary, had guaranteed that our depth at the quarterback position was going to take a hit.

Still, one thing I'll always admire about this Yearwood State team is their togetherness and ability to play as a team no matter what the circumstances.

They practiced hard that day, finishing with one of their best practices yet. Facing a team as inferior to us as Bethel Trinitarian, it would have been justifiable for our guys to "coast" and put forth less than full effort. Instead, they rallied around Jakobe in his return and played with intensity. The defense actually kept Jakobe and the offense out of the end zone during one of the scrimmages we had that afternoon, with Chris Whiteside picking off one of his passes in the end zone. Dennis Roberts, at nose guard, sacked him twice.

That said, Jakobe was not without his own moments, making throws on the run, and scrambling and gaining big yards with his legs when he could not pass downfield.

"Downtown" Mathias Brown ran hard and had several bruising carries that netted him big yards.

I was pleased with the effort.

I left practice in a good mood that afternoon. Which is why, as I got back to my office, I should have seen what was coming next.

Waiting outside was Denvis McBride.

"Afternoon, Coach," he said with a forced grin.

"Denvis," I replied.

"Got a minute."

"Let's go," I said, opening the door to the head coach's office, and ushering him in.

"I'm guessing this is about Charlie," I stated as I sat down behind my desk. On it were a few pictures and other things I had managed to take out of boxes after moving from my assistant coach's office and into Swicegood's old one.

Denvis sighed. "Just got off the phone with him. He's pissed... about Connor. Don't think I've ever seen or heard him as pissed as he was then."

"So am I," I responded. "I assure you it's the right decision, though."

"Yeah," Denvis affirmed. "And, Jayce, I'm not here to preach at you, and I'm not here to change your mind. I'm here because I care about you and I need to warn you about what you've done."

I studied him "Did Charlie send you?"

I studied him "Did Charlie send you?"

Denvis smiled. "No. But I expect he'll be paying you a visit in short order."

"I look forward to it," I responded, my eyes flashing.

Denvis was sympathetic. "Jayce, you've got a right to be angry. I know Charlie, and I know the Stinsons, and it doesn't surprise me in the least to learn that Connor Judd raped that girl, and that they set up Jakobe to take the fall. Nor does it surprise me that they're passing the buck and not taking responsibility. They're rich, white guys. It's what they do. The reason I'm here, though, Jayce, is to warn you."

"Warn me?"

"About picking a fight with Charlie Stinson."

"You think you're telling me something I don't know?"

"He'll get you fired," Denvis said, without batting an eye. "Jeff Swicegood's firing? It was as much about Charlie as it was about the angry women's groups."

"Meaning what?"

"Meaning it took more than a bunch of loud protests in our parking lots for Quinn Howser to finally pull that plug."

"Swicegood was fired because of donors pulling out of Yearwood State over the Jakobe news," I told him.

"And who do you think was responsible for convincing them to pull out?" Denvis looked me in the eye. "And once Swicegood went, who do you think got back on the phone with those same rich people and told them to stand pat, now that Jeff Swicegood was out of the picture?"

I took a deep sigh.

Denvis went on, "Charlie Stinson's been behind this whole mess, always pulling the strings; from what happened with Katie to all the drama surrounding Swicegood's firing. Fact is, he's probably one of the most powerful boosters in America, despite how small a school Yearwood State is. It shouldn't be the case, but it is. And as long as it is the case, then you probably need to think long and hard about what you've done this afternoon."

I got up from my desk chair, and stood at the window, over-looking the field. My thoughts were a jumbled mess.

"I know how you're feeling," Denvis told me.

"Do you?" I asked, skeptical.

"Yes," Denvis said. "You think that punk hasn't threatened me before? And I'm talking about my livelihood, and not just my status as booster club vice president. I've had to make these kinds of decisions, Jayce. And frankly, I'm not proud of many of them. But I love this university, and I love these kids. And I want to keep serving them. Unfortunately, the road to seeing that hap-pen runs right through Charlie Stinson's checkbook. Like I said, I know how upset you are about Katie. But you need to think bigger-picture here.

At this, I whipped around to face him. "Maybe it's you who needs to think bigger picture."

Denvis was taken aback at my response.

"Because where does it end, Denvis?" I continued. "How far do we let this kind of crap go on? You know, I didn't even rec-ognize Katie at Milo's funeral yesterday? She used to be one of those girls that would just brighten your day each time you saw her. And yesterday, she looked like she was walking under a cloud of death just so she could pay her final respects to a boy we all loved. What is that? How messed up do things need to get around here before we start taking the high road and demanding decency from everyone, and not just people that don't have the wealth Charlie Stinson does?"

Denvis had no answer.

"I'm not backing down from this, and I'm not letting up on Charlie Stinson. I'm gonna coach my team the way I coach my team."

I walked over to the door and opened it, signaling that it was time for him to leave. Denvis McBride rose from his chair and walked toward the door.

"I just hope you know what you're doing, Jayce," he told me.

"Of course, I know what I'm doing," I affirmed. "I'm getting my team ready to kick Bethel Trinitarian's ass tomorrow. And I hope you'll be there to watch it happen."

Denvis managed a faint grin, one that I tried to return, despite the tension that had materialized between us.

"Mustang pride," he told me, extending his hand.

I grasped his hand and shook it.

Chapter 19

Game Day: Bethel Trinitarian College at Home

I stood in front of the players in our locker room for a final talk before we took the field that afternoon against the Crusaders of Bethel Trinitarian.

"Guys, we've been through a lot," I told them.

At that moment, a lump came to my throat. I was suddenly fighting my emotions as my own words triggered my memory, causing me to relive everything.

"A lot's happened over the past couple of weeks; Swicegood, Milo, and now Connor. But you guys..." I paused and collected myself, "you guys have stayed together as a team, and you've worked your asses off to get to this point in the season."

I was speaking from the heart and it was the truth. In a real sense, my own family and this team were the only two real constants that I felt I had in my life at that time. All of the consternation and adversity I had faced over the past week had been alleviated by seeing those I loved and cared about most stay united and together—despite our collective heartache.

I went on for several minutes, giving last-minute encouragement to play hard, play to the whistle, avoid stupid penalties, and above all else, do your job. When I was finished, the guys jumped up and began shouting encouragement to each other and slapping shoulder pads and snapping on helmets; something they usually did just before we exited the locker room and headed to the field. Today, though, there just seemed to be more energy than usual.

It felt good.

We headed into the tunnel and got ready to run onto the field amid the cheers and yells of our hometown crowd. The noise was already reaching a fevered pitch as we formed a line with me at the front. For some reason, in that moment, I thought of Milo.

Turning back to face the team, I noticed once more the black patches with white lettering that were sewn onto each player's jersey.

Mustangs For Milo.

"Guys, don't forget!" I called out to the phalanx of players behind me. "Who're we winning this one for?"

"Milo!" "Milo, baby!" "It's all for Big Milo, y'all!" came the enthusiastic response.

Moments later, we burst out of the tunnel and took the field, ready for battle.

We had won the coin toss and would receive. Deon Flowers and Chris Whiteside were backed up to our goal line, ready for the kickoff. When the ball was kicked, Deon took it and ran up field for a solid return, almost to the thirty-five-yard line.

I stood in the huddle with the offense, dual-hatting now as both head coach and offensive coordinator. I went over the first play with them; a belly dive run play up the middle with Downtown.

As soon as I said it, Jakobe seemed to bristle.

"What is it, Jakobe?" I asked with some urgency.

"Coach, man, let us fly on that first play," he almost pleaded. "Send Deon deep, and let me throw it."

I glanced at Downtown, who shrugged. "It's cool," he said, without me having to ask him. "I'll still get my yards. Jakobe's back, let him have some love."

I smiled, amazed at the selflessness I was seeing. "All right. Jakobe, it's yours. Strong right, eagle's wing, on two."

We broke the huddle and Jakobe led the offense out onto the field.

I watched as the team got set. Bethel Trinitarian's players were big, but they were nowhere near as talented, quick, or well-coached as we were. And it soon showed.

Jakobe took the snap from center, dropped back, and pump-faked once.

At the same time, Deon bolted downfield, stutter-stepped, and completely faked out Bethel Trinitarian's cornerback who was covering him. He then accelerated again, leaving the defender five yards behind him.

On cue, Jakobe let loose a perfect spiral of a pass which floated through the air and sailed downfield. Deon caught in stride around Bethel Trinitarian's forty-yard line and took the rest of the way in for a touchdown.

Immediately, every member of the offense took off for the end zone to congratulate Deon, who jumped into the arms of one of our linemen. The crowd was ecstatic, and our sideline had erupted in cheers.

When Jakobe reached the sideline again, he gave me a huge hug.

"Thanks, Coach!" he said.

"Hey, it was a good call," I told him. "You made that one."

"Naw," Jakobe said, pulling back. "I mean, thanks for believing in me again."

I slapped his shoulder pad. "Shouldn't have doubted you to begin with," I said.

"You good, Coach."

The rout was on.

Three more highlight reel touchdown passes later (all from Jakobe, and two of them going to Deon), and we were ahead 28-0. By halftime, we had widened our lead to 35-0 when Adalius Bennett picked off a pass which he ran back for a score.

Toward the end of the third quarter, after Jakobe had run for a fifty-yard touchdown, I sat him and the rest of the first teamers on offense and defense. It was time for the second and third-string guys to have a shot. Bethel Trinitarian managed to put up seventeen points in the fourth quarter, but by then we had the game well in hand.

Travis McHenry played admirably in his first playing time of the season. He threw a strike to one of our scout team wideouts who took it down to the one yard line. From there, Travis sneaked in on a quarterback dive over center.

The final score was 49-17.

It was a great day, at least on the field.

Off the field would prove to be a slightly different story.

The euphoria was still palpable as we headed into the locker room. I walked right behind Downtown and Jakobe and was about to turn in, when someone grabbed my arm.

"We need to talk," Quinn Howser said to me, a grim expression tainting his features.

"About?" I asked, my mood undampened by his.

"Rephrasing," he backtracked, "Charlie wants to talk to you."

"Guess he's made a puppet out of you too, huh?"

"Now's not the time to get cute, Jayce, and I'm pretty sure you know it."

Chuckling in spite of myself, I replied, "What I know is that our football team just kicked ass out there with Jakobe Ackerman at quarterback, and not a damn penny of Charlie Stinson's money can change that. So yeah, let's go talk to the bastard."

Howser glared at me.

"Lead on," I told him.

Turns out, Charlie Stinson was waiting for us as Howser and I turned a corner that led into a dark corridor underneath the stadium.

"Well," he glowered at me as Howser and I approached. "Quite a game."

I returned the stare and said nothing.

"Jayce, I gave you a chance to rethink your decision about my nephew yesterday. And Denvis tells me you're sticking by it. That bothers me."

"Not as much as your nephew raping a girl bothers me," I retorted.

A faint smile came to the corners of Charlie Stinson's lips. "Yeah, I know," he said. "No sense in denying it at this point. Connor did what he did. It was stupid, and he probably should have had sense enough to stay away from that party altogether. My family—especially the younger generations—tend to not have as much sense as us older folks. And I'm not sure why, but maybe it's just a generational thing; weakening of the gene pool, whatever you want to call it."

He paused and took a step closer to me, as Howser stepped away. Stinson towered over me, and leaned in as if to intimidate.

"But it changes nothing, Coach Leonard," he said. "Connor and I did what we had to do; shift blame, pin it on the black boy, all of it. It was all us. And no matter what's happened since then, no matter what that girl told you; rape or no rape, Connor plays or you lose your job. It's that simple. You saw what happened to Jeff Swicegood. Do you think I'd hold back in doing the same to you if you don't play by the rules here?"

A deep voice came from behind Charlie. "He ain't playing by your rules." Denvis McBride stepped out of the shadows and joined us. "None of us are anymore."

Charlie turned and looked at Denvis, surprised, but with a confident smile. "Denvis, you should be at the after-party. Why are you here?"

Denvis shook his head. "I followed you here, because I knew you'd be hunting down Jayce and doing exactly what you're doing now."

"And what am I doing now?"

Denvis's massive frame tensed, as if ready for a fight. "Same thing you've been doing for years to me and everyone else around you; manipulating, threatening, strong-arming anyone who won't give you your way."

Charlie's demeanor hardened and he fixed Denvis with an ice-cold stare. I watched him, amazed at the stand he was taking.

"What would you know about any of that?" Charlie snarled in an indignant tone. "Haven't I been good to you? Given you a position in the association? Taken you in when every racist in this town said to cut you lose?"

"Every racist minus one," Denvis retorted, stepping to within an inch of his face. The two men were roughly the same height, and were toe-to-toe, like two boxers about to square off. "I ain't your Negro, Charlie; and you ain't going to treat me like I'm your black henchman anymore."

"You get your black ass out of my face, boy," Charlie hissed. "And don't you forget your place."

In a flash, Denvis's right hand shot up like a rocket in an uppercut and caught Charlie Stinson right where the chin meets the jaw. There was a sickening crack that echoed down the dark corridor, as Stinson's head snapped back and he toppled backward into the arms of a shocked Quinn Howser.

The swift, violent act had stunned all of us, including Denvis himself, who stood with his chest heaving as he stared down at the barely-conscious Charlie Stinson, whom he had just decked.

"You ever call me that again," Denvis warned, "And I'll show you the left one, too."

Howser was struggling to hold Charlie up, and looked like a parent trying to carry an overgrown child.

"Are you out of your mind?" Howser wailed in a nasal tone at Denvis. "You could have broken his neck with that blow! What kind of minister are you, Denvis?"

Denvis was massaging his sore hand as he grinned at the sight of the two of them. "I'm a New Testament minister with an Old Testament can of whoop-ass," he retorted. "It's time you knew that."

I gave an ecstatic chuckle as I watched Howser lower Stinson - fighting to regain consciousness - onto the ground.

Denvis turned to me. "You go," he told me, gesturing with his head toward the locker room. "Stinson ain't gonna bother you no more. I'm gonna see to that, especially during the next session of the boosters. I'm going to tell them everything, and once they hear about what he and his boy did to that girl, they're going to run him out on a rail."

"Sounds good to me," I said.

Howser was glowering at Denvis. "You do that, and you'll be out on your ass as quick as Charlie will be." He turned and fixed his gaze on me. "Or as quickly as Jayce is going to be if he doesn't fix himself."

"Fix myself," I laughed. Then I turned to Denvis. "Actually, Den, you don't need to tell anyone anything, because I'm going to use this press conference to fix everything and tell everyone the truth about what's been happening around here."

"You do that," Howser snarled at me, "and you're finished."

"Stinson's finished," I replied.

Howser had no response for this. Everyone was silent for a moment.

"Guess you'd better get to your press conference, huh?" Denvis finally said. "You've got some news to tell the press, don't you?"

"You bet your ass I do."

Chapter 20

Pangs of intense anxiety gripped me as I stood in front of the podium.

I was still wearing my khaki pants and sweat-drenched Yearwood State polo from the game. *The hard-working coach*, anyone who saw me might have surmised. What people didn't know, however, was that the sweat was partly from the nervousness I felt, combined with the adrenaline running through my system from the violence I had just witnessed.

"Good afternoon," I announced, clearing my throat. "And thank you all for being here. As you can imagine, I am very proud of the effort put forth by our team out there on the field today. Our guys on both sides of the ball performed extremely well, and the job they did on the field today against Bethel Trinitarian is a testament to their hard work and how well they've pulled together in the face of adversity over the past several weeks."

I paused and collected my thoughts.

"Our team's performance on the field is also a direct result of the superb efforts of our coaching and support staff. They also deserve a lot of credit for what you all saw out there today. We have great coaches, and we also have a great team of support personnel."

I took a long pause, and it was noticed. A few reporters and other bystanders seemed to glance around the room at each other, wondering what why I appeared to be stalling all of a sudden.

"In fact, we have what I would call a second-to-none support staff," I added. "Not only has our support staff helped our team, some of them—one of them, in particular—has done so probably more so than most. And instead of being rewarded with the appreciation and thanks and kindness that she deserves, she's been rewarded with perhaps the most foul treatment upon a human being that I've ever seen in my life."

The room was silent, save for the clicking of cameras and pens scribbling on paper. No one seemed to be breathing. All eyes were on me.

"I know this press conference is already taking an unexpected turn," I stated. "And I hope you all will understand that what I have to say in these next few moments is more important than anything I could say about the game."

I paused to let this sink in.

"I'm not going to say this young lady's name, because I don't want to drag her through the dirt. Suffice it to say, though, that her life has been absolutely dragged through the mud these last several weeks. She's been mistreated in the worst possible way that anyone could ever treat a woman."

I paused and let this sink in.

"Coach," interrupted a reporter, "is this a reference to the incident involving Jakobe Ackerman."

"Let me finish," I glared at him. "I need to finish what I'm about to say, and then I'll answer your question or questions, assuming they still need to be answered."

This shut him up.

I paused and took a breath before continuing. "The truth is that we've had a young woman on our support staff get sexually assaulted," I stated. "She was taken into a room at a party when she was too inebriated to consent or say no to what was happening to her, and then she was made to have sex against her will. Was it Jakobe Ackerman? Hell no. I'm here to tell you right now, today, that Jakobe Ackerman, my quarterback—a young man with a checkered history of his own—was innocent in that particular wrongdoing, even though he was falsely accused of it. Jakobe Ackerman, for all of his past problems, is a quality young man who has more than atoned for whatever sins he committed prior to coming to Yearwood State. And he did not rape this young woman like you all were led to believe he did. It was another young man who is no longer with our team, whom I dismissed yesterday."

I paused, and listened as the reporters came to life. *"Who was it?" "Was it Connor Judd?" "Did someone pressure the girl into falsely accusing Jakobe Ackerman?"*

"AND I WISH TO GOD…" I had to yell over the din of the press room, "that the story ended there. I wish that all it took to put an end to this garbage was me simply having to kick someone off of my team. But sadly, that's not how it works. Turns out that the young man who raped this girl is also pretty dang well-connected to a prominent member of our boosters. So much so, that this booster actually covered up what actually happened and set her up to accuse Jakobe Ackerman."

I paused again amidst the clicking of media equipment.

"Thankfully, this woman has a conscience, unlike her attackers, and came to me and my wife recently with the story of what actually happened to her. And I want you to know it's made me sick to my stomach to be a Yearwood State Mustang. You heard that right. I love this university; I played for this school; and I have some of the fondest life memories I'll ever have thanks to the years I spent here as a student athlete and now as a coach. But when I think that such a depraved thing could ever happen to one of our own YSU family members—especially at the hands of another family member—it honestly makes me ashamed to even wear the shirt I'm wearing right now.

"Sexual assault," I went on, "should never happen to anyone—let alone among family members of any sort. And I'm here to tell you today that the fact that it's happened right in our backyard—among our Mustang family—ought to anger the shit out of anyone."

Another pause.

"But even that," I continued, "isn't the worst of it. No, the worst of it is that as long as you're rich and well-connected, or related to someone who is, you can get away with just about anything, including sexual assault. That's just the stone-cold reality. Money talks in this business, we all know that. But unfortunately, it also silences. It drowns out the voice of the voiceless, and in this case, one of those voices belongs to a young woman whose world has been shattered. That's where we are today in the state of our program at Yearwood State University, I'm sad to say. The college that I've known and loved for so long, that I've served for several years now, this college, this program is now in the firm grip of a single individual who has enough money to buy his way—and those who kiss his ass—out of trouble, especially when they're the ones causing trouble.

"I've refrained from naming names up to this point, but it's time to say one name out loud—the name of the man whose name is all over this campus, and who unfortunately wields more power over this campus than any one person ever should have.

"I'm speaking of Charlie Stinson."

More clicking, more flashbulbs, more furious scribbling.

"Charlie Stinson's nephew, whose name I won't say out loud, raped a young woman on our support staff. Then – knowing she was strapped for cash - he enlisted the help of his uncle to cover it all up. They did this by offering the victim hush-money to help with her financial aid if she agreed to blame Jakobe Ackerman for what happened to her."

"Can you prove that this happened?" a reporter asked.

"There's proof," I said, suppressing the urge to grin at the thought of Katie's photo of Connor in the bedroom. "Once an investigation gets underway, possibly as a result of this press conference, proof will surface that Charlie Stinson and his nephew were responsible for what happened."

"Why bring this up in a press conference?" asked another reporter.

I thought for a moment before answering. "Because some things are more important than football," I answered.

At that moment, I felt hot tears coming to my eyes, which I discreetly brushed away. "And because we just buried a teen-aged boy by the name of Milo Crenshaw. That boy, with all of his health disadvantages, loved this school and this football team with all of his being. He ran for a touchdown—a mock touch-down—on that very field out there just a few short months ago. And that's all he ever wanted to do; just to be a part of our team, out of sheer love for us, and love of the game of football. So, to answer your question: *that's* why I'm doing this now. I'm doing what I'm doing because standing up for what's right, especially in the face of power, and those who abuse it, is more important than football. And if I can be about the business of doing that, then I can honor the memory of people like Milo Crenshaw. That's why I'm doing this."

With that, I was finished. The questions kept coming...about Stinson—was he being investigated, what actually happened, and so forth; about me—was I resigning as head coach of Yearwood State after only two weeks; about the program—were we facing sanctions, et cetera. Such questions were best left, I decided, to the sports information director at our school.

For my part, I had said what I came to say, and I was exhausted. I exited the platform from behind the dais, and left.

Predictably, my cell phone was blowing up by the time I was ready to exit the locker room after showering and changing. Grabbing my bag, it rang again, and I grinned as I decided to answer it.

"Jayce, what the hell?" Darcy DeMarr fussed on the other end. "I just saw the press conference. When did you know about Katie's rape charges being falsified, and when were you going to tell me?"

"I'm surprised Katie hasn't told you," I said, picking up my duffel bag and heading out.

"She needs to," Darcy fumed. "And we're going to need some help now that Charlie Stinson's been accused as an accessory."

"I agree," I told her.

"You know he's going to try to quash any investigation we do."

"You mean he'll have Quinn Howser quash it," I clarified.

"Damn spineless puppet," she cursed to herself. "So then I'll need to start making phone calls, get some heavy hitters on the line; national organizations that specialize in high-profile cases and aren't afraid to stand up to folks like this."

"Good luck," I told her. "You'll probably need it. Let me know how I can help."

"You've helped enough already, Coach Leonard," Darcy told me. "That press conference was something else. It took real courage for you to get up there and do that, even if it might mean your job."

"We'll see," I told her. "I honestly don't care if I get fired at this point. I had to do the right thing."

"Thanks, Jayce."

"Thank *you*," I told her, hanging up just as I exited the stadium.

A throng of supporters were in the parking lot, and many of them held up pennants, flags, and other Yearwood State memorabilia. Amidst the cheering and euphoric merriment of our victory and its aftermath, I tried to look for Dixie and Jamie.

"Coach!" a familiar voice called out.

I turned and saw Katie waving to me as she stood near a fence that separated the stadium property from the parking lot. She looked good; better than she had in months, in fact. Her hair was returning to its natural color, and was pulled back into a blonde ponytail. She also wore a Yearwood State sweatshirt and a pair of jeans; modest clothes, but nowhere near the oversized garments I had seen her wearing at the gas station that day on my way to Florida.

"They're over there," she motioned, pointing to where my family stood.

Moments later, I hugged my wife and son, both of whom congratulated me on my first home win as a college head coach. Katie stood nearby. The press conference was still fresh in my mind, and it soon occurred to me that few people outside of the stadium knew about what I had just said publicly, even though it was already hitting the airwaves and internet.

So, I told all three of them about my remarks to the media, which caused them to look at me with astonishment and no small amount of concern.

"I didn't name you," I told Katie, which caused her to become visibly more relaxed. "But I outed the shit out of Stinson, and the press pretty much knows that Connor's his nephew, so putting two and two together won't be hard."

"When can we see it?" Jamie asked, a wide grin spreading across his face.

"Soon," I told him. "Right now, I'm starving, though."

"Tootsie's?" asked Dixie.

"Let's do it."

Chapter 21

Despite it being game day, Max was able to seat us at the restaurant not long after we walked in. He congratulated me on the win, and showed us to our table.

Soon after we were seated, my cell phone rang. I glanced at the screen and grinned.

"Sup, Deke," I answered.

"Jayce, my dude" Deke Hudson began, "you have *no idea* the shit storm you've caused up here in my studio, bro."

"The press conference?" I asked.

"That wasn't no press conference," he laughed. "That was a sermon on why money needs to stay the hell out of sports, which it does, but still! Folks are going crazy over what you said."

"I'm guessing Sport News is prepping it for airtime now," I said, as Max set water and menus down on the table.

"Oh, you know we are."

"Gives us something to watch while we're eating at Tootsie's," I told him.

"Same place you were when I gave Jamie his shout-out earlier in the summer."

"That's the one."

"Maybe I should give you a shout-out this time around," he laughed.

"For?"

"For telling it like it is," he said. "You've always done that, though."

"Getting to be old hat," I replied. "Might not even be worthy of a shout-out anymore, huh?"

"Just keep doing what you do, fam," Deke told me. "I love you like a brother, and so does Mikayla."

"Saw her during my trip home. Did she tell you?"

"Yeah, she texted me after you left," Deke answered. "That reminds me: did you hear the latest out of Lake Barrow?"

"What's that?"

"Ahmad quit."

"Dang," I said, though it really wasn't a surprise to me.

"He wasn't long for that job," Deke said. "Sims County needs a new coach, though."

"Looks that way."

"Or maybe an old new coach," he said with a chuckle.

"You coming to a point?"

"Your ass is probably out of a job after today," Deke said, "and this new opportunity just opened up. I'd say God's trying to tell you something."

And for the first time, moving back home to Lake Barrow crossed my mind.

"We'll see."

"Spartan pride," Deke said.

"Spartan pride, Mustang pride," I said. "All the same."

"Long as you got pride," Deke said, just before we hung up. "And you've got that."

Max brought our food later, and we were just getting started when I looked up and saw a group of familiar faces headed in our direction.

Jakobe, Downtown Mathias Brown, Deon Flowers, Adalius Bennett, and Chris Whiteside had all entered the restaurant and were walking in the direction of another table, when Jakobe saw us.

"Oh, Coach Leonard!" he exclaimed as he led the group in our direction. Then, seeing Katie, he stopped.

A tension filled the air, as the two cast uneasy glances at each other; Jakobe standing with his friends, and Katie seated between Jamie and Dixie.

Moments passed, and no one—at our table or in the group of my players who had just entered the restaurant—had any idea what was about to happen.

It was Katie who broke the suspense. "Let me up," she whispered softly to Jamie, who was seated at the end of the booth we occupied. Jamie complied and rose up, allowing Katie to slide out of her seat and stand up. She then walked over to Jakobe

"I'm sorry," she said in a shaky voice. "I'm so sorry, Jakobe, for what I did to you."

Jakobe gave her an icy stare. "You damn near ruined my life," he told her.

"I hope you can forgive me," Katie told him, tears coming to her eyes. "I got carried away…"

"…about the money," Jakobe interrupted her, his features softening. "I know. I heard what Coach said."

At this, he held up his phone and touched the screen. Immediately, my press conference began playing. It had gone viral.

"We all saw it," Chris Whiteside said.

"Ain't gonna lie," Jakobe continued, not taking his eyes off of Katie. "I'm still pissed. But I also know a thing or two about forgiveness, especially from all the shit that happened back at Louisville. I had to get forgiveness from a lot of people, including the young woman I wronged. Truth is, a lot of those same people are still pissed at me." He paused and thought for a moment. "But I'll never forget what one of my coaches told me. He told me right before I left that 'forgiveness is a choice.' And I guess right now's the time for me to pay that decision forward."

Katie kept her eyes on him.

"Been missing my tutor," he said, with a half-smile.

"Hopefully your grades haven't slipped too badly," she said, looking up with a teary grin.

"They probably have," he answered. "Let's fix that soon as we leave here. My place?"

"You got it."

"So we're good."

They hugged.

The guys joined our table and we had a good time replaying the recording of the press conference. I got made fun of for how I looked on camera, but in all seriousness, the guys were impressed with my decision to go public about Charlie Stinson.

"Dude's an asshole, man," quipped Deon Flowers.

"Language," Dixie scolded with a smile as Jamie laughed.

"Hey, here it is!" Downtown Brown exclaimed, looking up and pointing to a nearby television.

Sure enough, a Sport News Network host was leading off with the backstory of my post-game press conference. This was new territory for me. Other than Jamie's shout-out from Deke several months back, Yearwood State had never made it into the prime-time slots. And yet, there I was moments later, plastered on big screens across the nation. I had gone viral on internet and social media outlets all throughout the afternoon.

The whole thing was surreal.

"Proud of you, babe," Dixie told me, putting her arm around me and rubbing my back. Jamie glanced over at me, his eyes glowing with pride.

"Coach, you da man," Adalius said to me after it was over.

The other guys agreed with him.

It all felt good.

When everyone had received their food and drinks, Jakobe stood up with his soda glass.

"A toast," he announced, "to Coach Leonard, the ballsiest head coach to ever coach the Mustangs!"

"Hear hear!" said the other guys, raising their glasses.

After the toast, it was my turn. I slid out of the booth and raised my glass again.

"Another toast," I announced, "to Milo Crenshaw."

Everyone got quiet as a slight pall fell over the group.

"To the boy – the young man– who taught us all more about purity and keeping things real and why doing the right thing is never out of style," I announced. "And he taught us right over there," I said, gesturing in the direction of the stadium. "So here's to Milo!"

"To Milo!" everyone called out.

After dinner I drove Katie back to campus, where she would meet Jakobe later that evening for a long overdue tutoring session.

"I'm kinda surprised," I told her as I walked her past the stadium and toward her dorm room. "Jakobe's usually wiped out after a game. Think he'll be up for studying College Algebra tonight?"

"Well," Katie said, almost ruefully. "Maybe we'll just hang out and watch football or something."

I chuckled. "Or something," I mocked.

Katie gave me a playful punch in the arm as we walked.

It was then that I saw a luxury SUV parked near one of the stadium entrances. It looked out of place.

I studied it for a moment, before realizing who it belonged to.

Sure enough, a moment later I saw Connor Judd emerging from a building across the street—one of our athletic dorms—carrying a cardboard box in his hands. Charlie Stinson walked behind him as they both headed in the direction of the SUV.

My blood ran cold and then began boiling.

Katie saw them too, and stopped dead in her tracks, her complexion going pale.

Shit, I thought.

"We can walk around," I told her. "Go a different route. Connor's moving out."

Katie fought to control her breathing as she kept her eyes on both of them, neither of whom had seen us yet.

"No," she finally said in a decisive tone. "No. I need to do this."

Then she began walking again, with me trailing behind. I watched her as she strode, her demeanor emboldened with each step. Connor soon spotted her as she approached, and froze as she got closer.

"What do you want?" he asked her, a faint sneer on his face, as he held the box in his hands.

Katie said nothing, and never broke stride as she closed to within inches of him. Connor began to recoil as she approached, but was not fast enough, and was carrying a box on top of that.

Once Katie was in striking distance, she reared back with her right foot and hoicked it upward, driving a forceful kick straight into Connor's testicles. He yelped in pain and dropped the box he was carrying. Its contents spilled out; football trophies from high school. One shattered on the ground.

Katie wasn't finished. She tilted his head up and unleashed a right cross into his jaw. This sent him sprawling backwards against his uncle's vehicle. Connor crumpled into a heap, with one hand on his groin and the other massaging his face.

"Hey, stop it!" Charlie Stinson pleaded, bolting over and trying to restrain Katie with his arms. She tore free, and bowed up again, as if she would attack him just as quickly as she had assaulted his nephew. At this, he backed down, cowed by Katie's aggressive posture.

At the sight of Katie's attack, I became alarmed, but soon calmed as I realized how short-lived it was. Katie had subdued Connor in seconds, and was holding off one of the most powerful and wealthy men I knew.

I could not help but chuckle.

"Bad day for you, huh, Charlie?" I asked, walking up behind Katie. "Punched out by a black dude, and then watching your nephew get neutered by a woman. Not a good day to be oppressing people, is it?"

"You get her out of here!" Stinson snarled, his dark eyes flashing at me. "And after that ridiculous press conference, you'd better lawyer up, too, Leonard! Because I'm coming for you. You think you know me? You've only scratched the surface of how badly I can hurt people. You're next on my list, Leonard! Believe me, you're going down!"

Maybe I was just tired after the game. Or maybe I really didn't give a shit. Whatever it was, at that moment, I just stared at Charlie Stinson and began laughing. This seemed to make him even angrier, but the message was clear; he was now rendered impotent.

Katie and I began walking away. "Going down, huh?" I said, as we passed him, leaving him standing next to his injured nephew. "See you at the bottom, Charlie Stinson."

"You okay?" I asked her moments later.

She glanced at me. She was still a bit shaken by the adrenaline rush, but there was a brightness in her eyes that had been missing up until a few minutes earlier. She answered, "Never better."

I smiled as we walked in silence.

"Are you afraid of getting sued?" Katie asked me moments later as we reached her dorm.

I shrugged as we stood outside her door. "Maybe."

"You don't look it."

"Maybe I'm not worried," I clarified. "I don't know."

"Yearwood State's definitely on the map now, thanks to you."

I chuckled. "Hopefully that will make finding a high-profile lawyer fairly easy, if it does come down to a lawsuit."

"Maybe so."

"In any case," I continued, "the question is, will you sue Stinson? Like I said, most good lawyers—especially if they want the exposure—would take up your case in a minute. Suing for damages could yield a hefty verdict."

Katie seemed to think it over. "I need to get my life in order first," she finally said. "Financial aid, and what not. I've spoken to Darcy, and there are scholarships for victims like me."

"No kidding."

"I could use all the help I can get."

"The right kind of help," I clarified for her, to which she gave a rueful smile.

"Yeah."

"Live and learn," I said. "Guess we've all learned something here lately."

"What have you learned?" she asked me.

I thought for a moment. "Mainly about keeping purity in the game I love," I said. "Milo taught me that."

She smiled.

"How about you?"

"The importance of help from friends," she said. "Instead of taking the easy way out. I hate to admit it, but Charlie Stinson helped teach me that."

I nodded. "Charlie's nephew is about to learn what an ice pack feels like."

She laughed.

"So, are you going to stay at Yearwood State? I heard your conversation with Deke earlier."

I shrugged. "Who knows?"

Katie smiled at me. "Keep it pure, wherever you go."

"You know it," I told her.

We hugged and I watched her go into her dorm.

EPILOGUE

MUSTANGS' SEASON ENDS IN PLAYOFF LOSS DISAPPOINTMENT

YEARWOOD JOURNAL STAFF WRITERS
Sunday, November 16, 2019

YEARWOOD

The Mustangs of Yearwood State University saw their hopes of advancing deep into the 2019 playoffs dashed on Saturday as they lost in the first round to Arlington College, 24-7, at Mustang Stadium. The defeat marked the second time this season that the Mustangs had fallen to the Dreadnaughts, as Arlington had defeated YSU earlier in the year during an away game loss.

Jakobe Ackerman led the offense for the Mustangs with a spirited effort. He scored the team's only touchdown on a ten-yard scramble, and finished the day having completed 10 of 25 passing attempts for 205 yards, no touchdown passes, and an interception.

Interim head coach, Jayce Leonard, said he was proud of his team's effort in the loss.

"The guys played hard," he said. "Sometimes you just come up short, but Arlington came ready to play today. I'm proud of our guys. It's been a wild year, but they persevered through a lot. I'll always remember this team for that."

LEONARD TO LEAVE YEARWOOD STATE
YEARWOOD JOURNAL STAFF WRITERS
Wednesday, November 19, 2019

YEARWOOD

Jayce Leonard, Yearwood State University's offensive coordinator who served as interim head coach in the 2019 season, has resigned. Reports say he has accepted a job at his high school alma mater, Sims County High School, in Lake Barrow, Florida. Leonard had previously coached there from 2003 to 2009, and starred at quarterback prior to that in the late nineties.

Leonard leaves following a 9-3 season at YSU, of which he himself had a record of 4-1 as head coach following the departure of longtime coach, Jeff Swicegood.

"I want to thank Yearwood State for the opportunity to coach," Leonard said in a prepared statement. "YSU will always be a second home to me and my family. This was not an easy decision, though it was made easier by the underhanded actions of a few individuals with too much power."

University and athletic officials would not comment on Leonard's cryptic remarks at the end of his statement, but only stated that, "Jayce Leonard's contributions to Yearwood State University are, and will always be, greatly appreciated."

INVESTIGATION LAUNCHED INTO NEFARIOUS BOOSTER ACTIVITY
YEARWOOD JOURNAL STAFF WRITERS
Monday, December 16, 2019

YEARWOOD

The Center for Justice and Public Safety, a nonprofit organization based in Lexington, has launched an independent investigation into allegations surrounding a high-profile booster of Yearwood State University's football program. In a preliminary news release, CJPS has stated that they have reason to believe that Charlie Stinson, president of the Yearwood State Mustang Boosters, went to great lengths to conceal the sexual assault of a female YSU student, to include paying her money under the table which, he told her, would go toward paying off her student loans.

The CJPS, which is not a government entity, will use its findings to make a recommendation to university officials as well as state law enforcement and justice officials as to how they might legally proceed against Stinson and others named in the investigation.

According to an unnamed state official, CJPS has been instrumental in years past with helping to bring about justice and resolution to a wide swath of cases across many different circumstances and situations.

STINSON OUT AT YSU BOOSTERS; MCBRIDE INSTALLED AS PRESIDENT
YEARWOOD JOURNAL STAFF WRITERS
Tuesday, January 28, 2020

Yearwood State University's Football Boosters voted unanimously on Monday to oust long-time president, Charlie Stinson, and replace him with another long-time fixture in the Boosters, Denvis McBride.

The decision comes amidst an ongoing investigation into whether or not Stinson paid a young woman hush-money to provide false information about a sexual assault case at the university back in the Fall. It also comes in the wake of a tumultuous season which saw one of Yearwood State's marquee players, quarterback Jakobe Ackerman, falsely accused of the assault. Ackerman was ultimately exonerated when first-year interim head coach Jayce Leonard held a now-famous post-game press conference in which he not only vouched for Ackerman's innocence, but fingered Stinson as the instigator behind the accusation.

Stinson could not be reached for comment.

McBride, on the other hand, had this to say when asked about his feelings on the decision:

"God's good. I'm very happy with the decision, and I am proud of the Boosters for taking the step they took, and putting their faith in me. It's a great day. Mustang pride!"

CJPS FINDINGS RELEASED

YEARWOOD JOURNAL STAFF WRITERS
Friday, February 14, 2020

The Center for Justice and Public Safety (CJPS) has concluded its investigation into the case of Charlie Stinson, a well-known former booster of Yearwood State University football. The investigation team has released a statement indicating that their "evidentiary findings point to multiple instances of flagrant manipulation and dishonesty, as well as bribery and coercion" in the case of Stinson, who allegedly bribed a college woman at YSU to alter her story about the sexual assault she endured at the hands of a Yearwood State player. The CJPS has submitted its findings to state officials, as well as the university, with the recommendation that "investigative and administrative action be taken."

University and state officials have yet to comment, and Stinson himself has refused to make any public statement.

HOWSER OUT AT YEARWOOD STATE
YEARWOOD JOURNAL STAFF WRITERS
Friday, February 21, 2020

Quinn Howser, has tendered his resignation at Yearwood State. The longtime athletic director, himself a former walk-on basketball player, resigned effective immediately following the release of a CJPS report concerning Charlie Stinson, a longtime YSU booster. While the report did not mention Howser directly, a university official was subsequently quoted as saying that, "the report highlights an unusually cozy relationship between one of our most senior athletic officials and our most prominent boosters, and that's a problem."

Howser was not available for comment.

STINSON SUED
YEARWOOD JOURNAL STAFF WRITERS
Monday, March 2, 2020

Troubles continue for Charlie Stinson, the longtime former booster of Yearwood State's football program, as he was served notice on Sunday that he is facing a lawsuit on behalf of an unnamed YSU student. According to sources, the young woman is suing him for allegedly coercing her to alter her story about a sexual assault that involved her back in late 2019.

The woman, who is unnamed, had no comment to give our sources, but a lawyer from Survivor's Rights Initiative, a nonprofit agency dedicated to seeking justice for victims and survivors of sexual assault, had this to say. "Justice is long overdue for my client, who has been victimized twice; once by her perpetrator, and then again by Charlie Stinson. We will be suing for damages, and she will have her day in court to face her abusers."

SWICEGOOD JOINS LEONARD AT SIMS COUNTY HIGH

BARROW TIMES
By Biff Kilgore
Monday, March 2, 2020

Jayce Leonard added a high-profile hire to his coaching staff on Sunday. In a prepared statement, Coach Leonard announced that Jeff Swicegood, longtime head coach and offensive coordinator at Yearwood State University, would be coming to our very own Lake Barrow to help coach our Spartan boys.

While this development may come as a surprise to some, the relationship between these two fine coaches is well-known to many. As many know, our Coach Leonard, whom we are thrilled to have back with us, played at Yearwood State and was actually recruited by Coach Swicegood.

And so, we welcome Coach Swicegood to our town, and wish him well as he coaches offense for the mighty Spartans!

Over Two Years Later

Neither Jamie nor Dixie had been especially excited at the thought of uprooting and heading south to the place we had at one time called home. After all, Jamie was thriving; he had won the starting quarterback job as a ninth-grader at Yearwood High, and had done better as a freshman than anyone else that his coaches could remember.

Still, after everything that had happened in Yearwood, we all came to the conclusion that it was time for a change. And so, my family had reluctantly agreed to go with me back to Lake Barrow, where it all began.

The Charlie Stinson drama certainly played a role. But deep down, I was ready for a change; sick of the politics involved in college football—even at a smaller school like Yearwood State. And honestly, I missed high school.

So, we moved.

Then COVID-19 wiped out Jamie's sophomore season, and my first season back at the helm at Sims County. We played only six games, winning one and losing five.

The next season was moderately better. We played twelve games, and went eight and four, losing in the second round of the playoffs. Still, everyone was excited because most of our players were coming back the following year and many, including Jamie, would be seniors.

Jeff Swicegood had actually surprised me when he accepted my offer to move to Lake Barrow and become my offensive coordinator. At first it was a bit awkward having my old college coach working in a position under me. But Swicegood wasn't bothered by it, and we kept things humorous as we went forward with it.

Then there was Matt Danforth, who—in addition to working for Jim Gill, still - also joined my staff on a volunteer basis and agreed to coach the defense.

Life's funny sometimes, and unpredictable.

I never expected to be back here, in my old hometown, where I grew up both as a kid and as a coach. I never expected to be coaching with the likes of Jeff Swicegood and Matt Danforth, of all people.

I certainly never expected to be working for Mikayla Hudson, my adopted kid sister who I used to let tag along with me and her brother, Deke.

And I never expected to work in the place again where my friend, Soul Rasheed, was killed by a gunman back in 2003. Sometimes the place haunts me; I'll get chills and relive memories, but God and time heal all wounds, and it's still great to be home. Mom, the Gills, and everyone else are still here, and so this is probably where we'll stay for a while, now that I've ventured out and seen the world some. Now that I've seen how the "glory" of coaching college ball can go sometimes, I suppose I'm ready to turn in my wandering shoes—or cleats—and make my old hometown my forever home finally. "What else could I want at this point?" is the way I look at it.

A state championship in year three, maybe?

Lake Barrow, Florida
Friday, December 16, 2022
Orlando Florida
State Championship Game
Sims County High School vs. Northwest
Florida High School

It was overtime, and we had the ball inside the ten-yard line. Fourth down.

Northwest Florida High School, a team out of Pensacola, was our opponent, and their defense had been stuffing us all night each time we had driven inside the twenty-yard line.

The tension was thick. We had come so far, but we still needed this score if we were going to leave Orlando with our school's very first state title in history.

Northwest Florida had just kicked a field goal, and the score was 17-14. Our field goal team was now on the field, ostensibly to kick a field goal and tie it up, thereby forcing a second overtime.

"I don't know, Jayce," Jeff Swicegood said to me from the press box through the headsets I wore.

"Me neither," I answered. "But we're doing it."

On the field, our senior kicker lined up behind Jamie, my son, also a twelfth-grader and our senior all-state quarterback.

Jamie held the ball for our field goal team, which is why the play we were about to run was perfect, at least in my mind.

As I watched Jamie kneel down, I had to smile.

It had been a long road to the state title.

I kept my eyes on Jamie as he crouched down with the rest of the field goal team.

We were currently 13-1, and were a play away from either 13-2 or 14-1 and a state title.

Jamie, like always, was a picture of focus. But then he did the strangest thing: he turned around, and glanced toward the sideline. I watched him, unsure of what he was doing. *Surely, he's not losing focus…that's totally unlike him.*

It was a bright, warm December day in Florida, and Jamie had played hard. He was covered in sweat, which had caused his bushy blonde hair to become matted and fall down into his face, so that he was constantly having to push it away.

And yet, at that moment, I watched as he pushed his hair out of his face, looked directly at me, and winked.

Looking back, it was as if Jamie was saying to me, "I got this, Dad."

The ball was snapped, and Jamie caught it. He planted it on the ground just as our kicker began running forward.

Then just as quickly, Jamie bolted upward, running to his left with the ball on the called fake.

Northwest Florida's players were fooled, but not for long, and soon they were tearing after Jamie in hot pursuit.

Jamie was a good runner, even if he wasn't a natural scrambler, like Jakobe Ackerman, who was now a reserve quarterback for the New Orleans Saints.

He had been working on his foot speed during the offseason, and to this day, I'm convinced that this preparation was the difference between how the final play of the state championship game went, and how it could have gone.

Jamie reached the sideline, turned the corner, and narrowly missed being caught by a defender. Two more were right behind the first, and Jamie would have been slammed to the ground by them had he not planted his foot, cut inside, and sprinted past them.

After he reached the five, he had one defender to beat, and Jamie dove around the three-yard line, stretching out his hands with the ball in them for the end zone.

The ball crossed the line just as Jamie was hit, and the referee held up his hands.

Touchdown!

The 2022 Sims County Spartans had won the first-ever state title, 20-17.

Our sideline erupted, and most of the town of Lake Barrow – which had made the trip to Orlando - began emptying out of the bleachers and storming the field. There were tears, hugs, photos, tackling, and an ice bath for me as a cooler was dumped over my head.

Dixie found me and jumped into my arms, her face stained by tears of joy, makeup, and face paint, as she had decorated her cheeks with Jamie's "#7" jersey number.

"Thank you!" she yelled in my ear as she kissed it.

"For what?" I asked her.

"For moving us here," she said, squeezing me.

"Thanks for coming with me," I answered, tightening my own grip on her. "And for staying with me."

"Always."

I then found Jeff Swicegood and Matt Danforth, my two coordinators, and hugged them both. After this, I made my way around the field congratulating various players. Several of them had dads and other relatives whom I had played with as a player during my quarterbacking days at Sims County, and a handful of them came over to congratulate me.

Jim and Jacqui Gill had made the trip—in their RV of course—and found me on the field. They hugged me and Matt Danforth both.

Mikayla Hudson, our principal, was whooping and hollering and running around hugging and kissing everybody within reach.

I also congratulated as many Northwest Florida players as I could find, along with their coaches. They were subdued, but showed good sportsmanship. They had played hard, and I told them I was proud of their effort.

I didn't see Jamie, but I knew we'd have some time together later.

Sure enough, after all the festivities—mainly the trophy presentation on the field - it was time to load the buses and head back to Lake Barrow, just a short drive away.

The three of us - Jamie, Dixie, and I - sat together in the front seat of our bus, and looked at my phone.

Text messages were pouring in, and we basked in the love of our loved ones.

"So, so, so proud of you all! Yay! Go Spartans!" – Love, Mama Freddy (and Max, who typed this for her).

"Proud of you, Coach L. Geaux, Spartans! New Orleans sends love!" – Jakobe.

"Go Spartans! Proud of you, fam! Give my love to the boys!" – Ahmad (Coach Floyd)

"Sports News Network crew sends its love to Sims County! Tell your principal to give you a raise. That's an order from her big bro." - Deke

"Proud of you, Jayce (and the Sims County Spartans). Yearwood Boosters sends its love! Remember: think Big Picture!" – Denvis

"Oh, babe, you'll want to see this one!" Dixie exclaimed, handing me her phone with a smile.

I took it from her and looked at the screen.

"So proud of you all! Miss you! Congrats on the state championship! We're close to taking Charlie Stinson for all he's worth! Send prayers!" – Katie

I smiled and handed the phone back. "'Bout time for to Stinson pay up."

"Any word from him?" Swicegood asked from the seat behind me.

"Yeah," I replied. "He said congratulations, and he's sorry for getting you fired."

"Bull shit," Swicegood hissed.

I laughed.

"Any word on whatever happened to Connor?"

I shrugged. "Probably working for his uncle."

"Until they go bankrupt," Swicegood said with a chuckle.

"Hey!" Dixie chimed in. "No more of that talk. No negativity."

"Yeah, Dad," Jamie said. "Stop ruining the moment."

"Sorry."

It was the last text message that about did me in.

"Jayce, I cannot express how proud I am of you, son. Life has knocked you on your ass for years, but you always come back stronger and more determined than ever to do the right thing. And it's paid off. You earned this championship; you, my precious grandson, and all those boys on the field today. Enjoy every minute of it, and cherish it for the rest of your life. I love you." – Mom.

"You okay, Dad?" Jamie asked.

"Fine," I said, wiping my eyes. "Just pollen."

"In December?" Jamie asked.

"Don't be a smart-ass," I said, knowing my gig was up and showing him the text from his grandma.

He smiled as he read it.

"Lot of folks love us, huh?"

"What's not to love?" Jamie asked.

"Enough emotion," I said, "any thoughts on college?"

Jamie shrugged and gave a wry grin. "There's always Yearwood State."

I grimaced. "Why would you do that to your mother and me?"

He laughed.

"Seriously?" I pressed.

"I don't know," Jamie answered. "It's an option."

"So is Florida," I said. "And Central Florida. And Florida State, and USF. All well within a day's drive, and all of whom have offered you, bud."

"We'll see," he said. "Yearwood State worked out pretty well for you."

"As a player."

"Exactly."

"Just promise me you won't ever coach there."

"Only if you coach with me."

"Then no deal."

He laughed.

The bus rolled on. Soon, Dixie and Jamie both fell asleep on either side of me and were both snoring against my shoulder. I scanned my phone while they slept and soon grew tired of all the sports talk. Truth was, I was exhausted myself, and ready to doze off. But I kept scrolling and soon decided to look at my saved pictures.

I found an old folder which I had uploaded from a computer some time ago, and had then forgotten that it existed. It had over a hundred old, scanned photos in it and I spent a few minutes reliving memories from years past.

There were photos of Jamie's little league days; pictures of him and Milo; and plenty of others taken over the years; family events, football banquets, trips, and the like. A few pictures of Soul appeared, and I found myself wishing that somehow, he could be here for this moment.

Soul Rasheed had come to Lake Barrow years earlier to coach with me, and had fought to find his place in our small town. In my mind, he deserved to celebrate this win as much as anybody.

Some things in life just aren't fair, and at that moment, I wished that I could somehow at least get a text from him also… something that would allow us to share in the moment together.

I kept right on scrolling, but stopped when I came to a video that had also found its way into that old, forgotten digital folder.

It was a video of Soul; one from that first season, our first season, at Sims County way back in 2003. It was during preseason workouts, not long before our first game.

Soul was speaking to our players on the practice field.

"I promise you, guys, I promise you," he was saying, *"there's not much that can compare with running out onto that field out there right before the game starts. That game-day atmosphere is electric, and make no mistake, it's a privilege to be able to be a part of it. It's the only place—maybe other than your place of worship, if you have one—where the human experience is at its purest. It's a sanctuary, a sacred place. Never forget that."*

"Never forget that," I whispered to myself.

"What, babe?" Dixie asked, waking up.

I showed her the video, and we watched it together, listening to Soul's words. As the video played, I remember thinking that somehow, maybe this was his way of reaching out to me—from somewhere off in the eternal realm—and giving me his best wishes on a day that was meant to be shared by both of us.

I smiled, and Dixie looked at me with tears in her eyes.

"He was there today," she told me.

I felt a lump come to my throat as I glanced out the window, and watched the scenery go by as the bus rolled on its way, carrying us back to Lake Barrow.

Back to our home.

"Right where he should be," I said. "With the rest of us."

www.ingramcontent.com/pod-product-compliance
Lightning Source LLC
Chambersburg PA
CBHW031503120626
46545CB00005B/1724